To Dr. John White (1924–2002):
father-in-law, mentor, friend.

Contents

Acknowledgements

I owe an enormous debt of gratitude to the faculty members of ACTS Seminaries (Trinity Western University's graduate school of theology) who, through their thoughtful championing of Word and Spirit, helped to hone not just my craft but my character. A specific acknowledgement is due to Randy Wollf, Ph.D., Associate Professor of Practical Theology and Leadership Studies at MB Seminary; and to Dirk Büchner, D.Litt., Professor of Biblical Studies at Trinity Western University. Gentlemen, your encouragement has meant the world to me.

Many thanks to my colleagues at MULTIPLY (formerly MB Mission) who weekly give so generously of their time to discuss nuances of text and push relentlessly for clarity and economy of words. That my writing is worthy of publication at all - much less of a book award - is because you have helped make it so. It is pure joy to work with such an outstanding, quirky team of creatives and missionaries who are determined to make Jesus the hero of every story.

I'm immensely grateful to the editorial team at Word Alive Press, particularly to project manager Marina Reis and editor Kyla Neufeld, for their invaluable support and guidance. Ladies, you have gone above and beyond.

Thank you, friends and family members, for tolerating my incessant and invasive forays into your private lives, and for allowing me to write your personal stories of challenge and redemption. A special note of thanks to my husband Scott, and to my children John, Robin, and David. You are God's poems, and it is an honour to be part of the cadence of your lives.

"Challenging, exploratory, humorous, painfully honest, Nikki White's revealing penetration into the life of Moses, Old Testament hero and human being, speaks to those of us who feel we have lost our way in the exile of contemporary life, asking the questions that lie at the heart of true human identity. We may think we know the story of Moses, but in these pages, he comes to life in such a vivid, compelling way that we begin to hear God's voice challenging Moses and us. Read this book and give it to your friends."—*Luci Shaw, writer-in-residence at Regent College and author of numerous books, including* The Crime of Living Cautiously *and* The Generosity

"If anyone should have been confused about his identity, it was Moses: prince, shepherd, Egyptian, Hebrew. Instead of allowing himself to be paralyzed by self-doubt, discouragement, or fear, he instead chose to answer the call of God. Nikki White's powerful and relevant book, *Identity in Exodus*, shows how we can answer that call too. We need not search for our identity in the wrong places, or allow other people, our past, or harsh circumstances to define us. With Moses as our role model, we can know the fulfillment of becoming one of God's Sent Ones."—*Dr. Joseph Bentz, professor of English at Azusa Pacific University and author of* Nothing is Wasted

"With skillful storytelling born of experience and vulnerability, Nikki White weaves a tapestry of the human Self, including the best and the false identities we assume, and shows us that to be clothed and called by God makes us who we intrinsically are. Moses, friend of God, moves in and out of her narrative. He is the pattern for all characters summoned to do God's work (including Jesus) and becomes a close companion to we readers who have experienced the precarious nature of life, and who struggle against prevailing culture and find ourselves to be strangers in a strange land."—*Dirk Büchner, professor of Biblical Studies at Trinity Western University*

"'Who am I?' It's the most fundamental question that any of us can ask. By joining Nikki White in her literary journey plumbing the life of Moses, we find helpful hand grips for our own journey to define ourselves. Acceptance, belonging, and security are anchored in God and realized through the lens of scripture. *Identity in Exodus* will challenge and surprise you, and it will ultimately comfort you to know both *who* are and *whose* you are."—*Dr. Rick Franklin, Vice President, Arrow Leadership*

"After thirty years of engagement with thousands of short-term and long-term participants in cross-cultural mission, I wish this book had been available for all of us years ago. Navigating the challenges of identity in cross-cultural service and our sense of purpose in life requires candour, honesty, and fearlessness. Nikki White writes with prophetic clarity, courageous personal vulnerability, and a deep respect for God's timeless truth. This book is for anyone who wants to be honest about facing who they are, whose they are, and where they are going."—*Randy Friesen, D.Min., General Director, MB Mission/Multiply (2004-2021)*

"Nikki White is a skilful writer, a great wordsmith, and an insightful thinker. She brings to life the story of Moses, showing how his journey is relevant to the average person who is grappling with their sense of identity and calling in these challenging times. Real-life stories of her own struggles and those of many others bring this book alive."—*Andy Park, musician, songwriter, and author of* To Know You More

"Following the story of Moses, and drawing from her own personal story, Nikki White shows how 'glorious misfits' can move from identity crisis to a life of missional community. *Identity in Exodus* weaves through the messiness of community and offers a beautiful picture of the Body of Christ that is vulnerable, authentic, and anchored in love for one another. This book gives me hope that we can actually encounter God if we would just stand still before the burning bush together."—*Matthew Price, Senior Pastor, North Langley Community Church*

"There are few topics today receiving more attention that the current discourse on identity. Academic understandings arise out of both the psychological and sociological influences of identity formation. But as Christians, we understand that there is a transcending voice that declares who we are—the voice of God. Nikki White, in a beautiful and skilful way, explores this transcending voice through the life of Moses, incorporating her own story and those of others to bring the identity discussion into practical and personal terms. I know you will enjoy and be led to and through this important discussion in *Identity in Exodus*."— *Dr. Rob Rhea, Associate Vice-President, Trinity Western University*

"I highly recommend Nikki White's *Identity in Exodus*. This book will encourage those of you who feel like misfits: not fitting in with either secular culture or evangelical 'church-ianity.' White's thoughts regarding the toxic strategies that we employ to discover and define our identity are insightful and gospel centred. Her use of Moses, the children of Israel and Exodus as the metaphor for this journey of identity is compelling. In a world of racial division, pandemics and radical individualism, White has called us back to a powerful identity in Christ and his body."— *Dr. Bill Taylor, Executive Director, Evangelical Free Church of Canada*

"*Identity in Exodus* is an insightful and well-articulated assessment of the paralysis of identity crisis that plagues much of Western culture. White beautifully weaves the biblical story into the blended narrative of identity and mission in a way that makes Moses relevant and relatable, like one of us, on the same journey to find our true home with God himself. *Identity in Exodus* is a great resource for those who have experienced, are experiencing, or will experience (and you will) significant life uncertainty and transition."—*Dr. Mark Wessner, President, Mennonite Brethren Biblical Seminary*

"Year ago, I had the privilege of reading Nikki White's early thoughts on the role of identity in leadership. I commented, 'This must go beyond you and me!' I am thrilled that she has taken those outstanding preliminary ideas much further in *Identity in Exodus*. White's creative and engaging storytelling will warm your heart, make you laugh, and bring tears to your eyes, as she masterfully weaves stories together with the Moses narrative, showing how the most humble man on Earth came to find his identity in exodus. My hope and prayer is that you, too, will recognize God's mission for your life—a divinely orchestrated exodus—and find identity as his Sent Ones."—*Dr. Randy Wolff, associate professor at MB Seminary and author of* Maximum Discipleship in the Church; Navigating Church Politics

"Disarmingly vulnerable, authentically worshipful, this is a book for the honest majority who struggle with identity and calling. Nikki White draws us into the searching journeys of a multitude of biblical characters, and makes a convincing connection to Moses, not as the great liberator, but as the great struggler who is just like you and me. White's masterful storytelling illustrates deep truths, extracting extraordinary wisdom from the seemingly ordinary events of our daily lives."—*Victor Wiens, author of* Refugees and Ambassadors: Mennonite Missions in Brazil

"With casual brilliance, Nikki White lifts the lid on tough and timely questions regarding identity, probing into the life of Moses for vital insights. If you have struggled with your sense of calling, this book will help you connect with your true identity, through identifying more deeply with those to whom God sends you."—*Dr. Paul Beckingham, psychotherapist and author of* Walking Towards Hope

IDENTITY
IN EXODUS

Journey with Moses from Identity Crisis into Missional Community

NIKKI T. WHITE

IDENTITY IN EXODUS
Copyright © 2021 by Nikki T. White

Unless otherwise indicated, all scripture quotations taken from The Holy Bible, New International Version® NIV® Copyright © 1973 1978 1984 2011 by Biblica, Inc. TM. Used by permission. All rights reserved worldwide. • Scripture quotations marked KJV are taken from the Holy Bible, King James Version, which is in the public domain. • Scripture quotations marked ESV are taken from The Holy Bible, English Standard Version® (ESV®) Copyright © 2001 by Crossway, a publishing ministry of Good News Publishers. All rights reserved. • Scripture quotations marked NASB are taken from the New American Standard Bible®, Copyright © 1960, 1962, 1963, 1968, 1971, 1972, 1973, 1975, 1977, 1995 by The Lockman Foundation. Used by permission. • Scripture quotations marked NKJV are taken from the New King James Version®. Copyright © 1982 by Thomas Nelson, Inc. Used by permission. All rights reserved.

The content of this publication is based on actual events. Names may have been changed to protect individual privacy.

ISBN: 978-1-4866-2061-6
eBook ISBN: 978-1-4866-2062-3

Word Alive Press
119 De Baets Street Winnipeg, MB R2J 3R9
www.wordalivepress.ca

WORD ALIVE
—P R E S S—

Cataloguing in Publication information can be obtained from Library and Archives Canada.

Invitation to the Reader

Moses was a misfit. And, within the Western Church, he has many his kindred spirits. Millennials, migrants, ex-missionaries, shamed souls, the socially awkward, and more—we populate the crowded societal fringe, uncertain of how to fit into a complex and nuanced world. Ours is an identity in constant crisis, at times leaving us feeling isolated, confused, or purposeless. Yet, like the prophetic patriarch of the Old Testament, we misfits have much to impart to those who might otherwise live safe but shallow lives, tucked away in a comfortable cocoon of spiritual complacency. Misfits serve to remind the Church that it is not upon this Earth for the sake of pillage, but pilgrimage. Or else, the Bride of Christ may find herself far too much at ease in her exile, forget her mandate altogether, and realize that her need to find comfort in the familiar, left unchecked, smothers the soul.

Do you struggle with a sense of Self? Have you gone through a transition that left you adrift, doubting your vocation and your value? Are you overwhelmed by the myriad of choices in the world and our culture's insistence that you alone must decide which competing emotion defines your most authentic Self? Have trauma, abuse, neglect, or shame paralyzed you in your pursuit of purpose? Hear this: there is cause for great hope. Read on and learn how God desires to use you to inspire a drowsy Church with much-needed, divine discontent. You have a high calling, and you are not alone. You have, in fact, excellent travelling companions. I invite you to come on a journey with Moses, finding identity in exodus.

Wanderer, come out of the wilderness. You are being *sent*.

CHAPTER ONE
The Call

No one can lay greater claim to identity confusion than Moses. By eighty years of age, Moses had been immersed in three distinct cultures without ever fully belonging to a single one. The elderly Hebrew-Egyptian-Midianite had, by this point in his lifetime, worn the clothing of prince, slave, hero, criminal, and shepherd. He had lost whatever tenuous confidence he once had in identifying with any people group whatsoever, despondently naming his own son "Stranger" during his self-imposed forty-year exile in the desert.

Then, in the midst of his resignation to a fate of obscurity on the arid plains of Midian, Moses hears someone calling his name. Before the burning bush, Moses was confronted by the God of his ancestors, a God who asks of him the unimaginable: "Go."

The call comes far too late. Forty years previously Moses had tried, and failed miserably, to be the rebel leader of his oppressed people. Now he's an old man, full of regrets and resignation. But the call is clear: "... *Go. I am sending you to Pharaoh to bring my people the Israelites out of Egypt*" (Exodus 3:10). Not surprisingly, Moses flinches. The depth of his angst is clearly seen in his reply. "*Who am I,*" he asks, "*that I should go to Pharaoh and bring the Israelites out of Egypt?*" (Exodus 3:11). Those first three words form the question that Moses likely asked himself all of his life. Who *am* I?

How many of us have asked ourselves that same question?

Like Moses, we may struggle to define ourselves when buffeted by an intolerable pace and process of change. Overwhelmed, we find refuge in whatever is most familiar, even if the familiar is a numbing surrender to our own namelessness, self-medicating through whatever distractions are most accessible to us. Career, sex, money, substance use, romance, gaming, self-expression, family roles, and social media are all good in and of themselves, but they can become perilous to those who use them to ignore the discomfort that comes with facing these most unsettling existential question: Who am I? What is my purpose? Why am I here? Without answers to these questions, we have no way to integrate traumas and crises into the truest overarching narrative of God's story for our lives. Worse still, by stifling these questions, we eventually stop caring. Divine discontent, meant to drive us toward God, is incompatible with self-sedation.

Secular wisdom tells us that answers come from within, that we must dig deeper into our own desires. Canadian philosopher Charles Taylor, exploring modern identity in his book *Sources of Self*, writes that we have become a "society of self-fulfillers."[1] He points out that Western culture now revolves around the primary values of self-expression, self-realization, self-fulfillment, and authenticity. The latter, society tells us, requires that we define ourselves according to our core desires, a daunting, if not impossible, task. How do we pull identity out of the tangle of conflicting, inconsistent, and ambiguous human desires? The deep-seated human desires for security, significance, and love are constant. Secondary desires—for those things we are convinced will make us *feel* secure, significant, and loved—are transient. Those secondary desires, and thus the life goals they inspire, change from week to week, mood swing to mood swing. Do I want freedom or intimacy? Safety or adventure? Traditional or non-binary sexuality? Autonomy or community? Do we defer to the spontaneous burst of one powerful emotion, or the most recurrent? What of those emotions that are so nuanced—or so turbulent—that they are incomprehensible in the

---

[1] Charles Taylor, *Sources of the Self: The making of the Modern Identity* (Cambridge, MA: Harvard University Press, 1989) 508.

moment? If our emotions are to lead the way in discerning our identity, then which one do we adopt? Which self is our truest self?

It can be crushing to be told that we alone bear the burden of self-identification based on discovering our most authentic desires. Consider, for example, that anxiety and depression among young adults in developed countries has reached an unprecedented high. Could it be because youth are told to pursue a life path that fulfills their heart's desires? But which desire? Overwhelmed, many are paralyzed by indecision. If they manage to choose from among their many desires and forge a path toward its fulfillment, they may find that success does not satisfy. Life is full of disappointments. Where previous generations might have expected that disappointment and handled it with a certain pragmatic resilience, this generation may find it unbearable. In the face of such disillusionment, we have limited options: get bitter, get busy, or get stoned. Gripped by a sense of bitter victimization, we may choose to blame others ("You are failing to fulfill me"), blame society ("This social system is failing to fulfill me. I am perpetually outraged"), blame ourselves ("I am failing to find fulfillment; I am a loser"), blame God ("God, you are failing me—the deal is *off*"), or simply give up ("There is no such thing as fulfillment; Nietzsche and Buddha were right.").

Rather than get bitter, we may instead get busy. In this case, we cope with disappointment by becoming competitive hyper-achievers, busy "getters-of-things-done" who live for the next accomplishment, achievement, or victory. In this state, we are likely to frequently change or discard relationships, careers, or values, hoping that our next choice will somehow provide that elusive sense of personal fulfillment we're missing.

Failing this, we may choose to get "stoned," letting disappointment lead to self-medicating through various means as we exchange the possibility of joy and meaning for the more reliable solace of pleasure.

What then? Is there another option?

There is one who calls to us, whose words can set our hearts thrumming in a way that none of our own desires ever can. For our defining moment, we must look not within, but outside of ourselves. Moses had no way of knowing that the trajectory of the trauma in his life would lead to him becoming the founder of a new, divinely-inspired culture. He had, as we shall see, justifiable cause to wrestle with self-doubt, anger, ambition, sin, bitterness, regret, despair, and aching loneliness. It is no surprise that he hesitated at the bush and argued with God regarding this calling. The resurrection of hope is painful, like blood flowing into a limb when its circulation has been cut off. Moses could not envision how the crises of his past would in fact uniquely equip him to confront the abusive authority of a pharaoh, to disrupt the defeatist passivity of an enslaved people, and to lead a nation of malcontents out of exile through a forty-year exodus into their destiny. Moses did *not* see that coming. So, it is highly likely that we, too, underestimate the call of God on our lives.

Let us not underestimate the Caller. Our God is the one who sovereignly disturbs the status quo, awakens us to the folly of self-actualization, and dares us to look not in, but up. Our feeble protest is drowned out by the imperious thunder of his call. Who am I, you cry, that you should send me? Who are you to refuse? We who refuse to go willingly where God is sending us will go inadvertently somewhere else—swept up into an inexorable wave of involuntary migration and dumped upon some unfamiliar shore, disoriented, undignified, and afraid. Either way, change is inevitable. We all go somewhere, whether we want to or not. The challenge lies in our willingness to stand before a burning bush, embrace the disruption of God's call, and allow it to re-shape our fragile sense of Self.

CHAPTER TWO
Who Am I?

BLESSED ARE THE MISFITS

"I could tell right away that I wasn't fitting in," Michael said. "But, by then, I had learned to expect it."

Though born on the mission field in South America, Michael had lived in six different countries by the time he was ten years old. Each move brought a fresh crisis. "I would just get used to one country and start to figure out the social cues. Then we would move again." He shook his head. "It felt hopeless."

Eventually, the family moved to North America. This was familiar territory to his parents, but the children with whom Michael tried to play had little in common with the Latinos of his childhood. By the time that Michael was a gawky pre-teen, he felt utterly alone, handicapped by his clumsy attempts to fit in with North American fashions and idioms. His face reflected the grim pain of those memories as he told his story.

"I lost myself during those years," he recalled. "Who was I? I was the lonely son of former missionaries; other than that, I had no idea who I was." He smiled faintly. "Fifty years later, and I'm still not sure."

***

Michael is what is referred to as an "MK" (missionary's kid). His parents, although eager to help him adapt to Western culture, were themselves suffering from the inevitable identity crisis faced by missionaries who leave the field and decide to come "home," only to find that "home" is frustratingly elusive. Despite the fact that his family stayed in North America, Michael remained insecure in his identity for most of his life, with few friends. He sank into a clinical depression in his early twenties.

Church provided some sense of belonging, but even there Michael encountered the subtle nuance of social caste distinction between those who were confidently woven into the fabric of the local Christian culture and those whose loose threads marked them as outsiders. The family uprooted and moved multiple times within North America, each move causing Michael to feel himself thrust further out into the isolated fringes of society.

Michael and his parents, as ex-missionaries, were experiencing culture shock. Like immigrants who leave their birth country for foreign shores, this family experienced genuine trauma, particularly when faced with the daunting prospect of integrating into the sophistication of Western culture. They faced the obstacles of finding employment and adapting to a sudden drop in social standing. The sense of insignificance was overwhelming. Michael's family expected to experience this trauma when they first arrived on the mission field, but they were unprepared for the equally traumatic experience of re-entry. Leaving behind a long-established ministerial role (with little secular merit) left them helplessly adrift when they returned to their country of origin. They were neither fish nor fowl, their core sense of significance gone. By definition they were "misfits"—displaced persons with difficulty integrating into a society.

These ranks are growing at an alarming pace in Western cultures. In fact, one might even say that misfits are going mainstream. Let's consider a few examples.

We've already mentioned millennials, who feel forced to choose the One Right Path among innumerable options or else suffer eternal insignificance. More and more, they are relegated to the fringes of society by their own inability to make the decisions that would help them integrate. This is made worse by the pace of technological advancement. In the four years required to complete most undergraduate degrees, job requisites may suddenly change to fit with new advances in the field, or entirely new fields unfold. Generalized disciplines of study are now insufficient to land a job, and a competitive market demands that the decision to specialize must be made as early as high school: the most agonizing and confusing phase of puberty.

Social media, ironically purposed to bring a greater sense of connectedness, has made misfits of all but the most confident and accomplished among us. While explosively expanding our universe, it also cripples us with image anxiety. We frantically scramble to stay atop of the latest memes, life-hacks, and acronyms used by the Hive Mind. We cower as we are mercilessly lectured, feeling condemned if we do not "Like" the latest rant of moral or political outrage. Media pushes upon us its own definition of racism, deems gender and gender identity to be fluid, dismisses religious traditions as irrelevant, and insists that true community—and true love—are more easily found online, rather than in actual face-to-face encounters. Dare to disagree? You are a misfit.

Then there are aging misfits, whose plight is similar to that faced by new immigrants. Like them, we face the intimidating challenge of transitioning to a new definition of Self. We are expected to untangle complex cultural codes of a society in constant flux. How can we possibly keep up with the pace of change? Today's knowledge and skill may be tomorrow's sneer. Like new immigrants, we feel a sense of inadequacy along with a radically diminishing social status, made much worse as we age. As middle-aged weariness creeps in, we are prone to stop trying to fit in altogether. We may withdraw to a moral high tower from which we critique and criticize society and nurse an obsessive sentimentality about the Good Old Days. From there, we pretend that our isolation is, in fact, by our own choice.

Misfits often feel victimized. When we are forced into a context in which we do not feel comfortable, it's as if we are being deported, displaced, or kidnapped. Certainly, this was the case with Michael's family, and especially with his mother. She felt like a refugee, neither called nor sent, just banished. She lost the vital sense of significance she experienced on the mission field and felt disheartened and empty while contemplating life amongst the fattened sheep of the global North. As the years passed, she felt increasingly resentful. For a time, she took on an assumed air of martyrdom, seeing herself as a noble but undervalued hero who had now become a misunderstood, marginalized victim. She became Batman.

I AM BATMAN

In today's climate of political polemic—with social media heightening both our awareness of divisive social issues and, in some cases, escalating them—victimhood is almost trendy. Even the entertainment industry, in promoting superhero movies, persuades us there are only two desirable identities: The Hero and the Victim. In many cases, the superheroes we admire most are also victims, tragically misunderstood and mistreated. Increasingly, young people are being drawn into a romanticized identity in which being a victim is their primary and even preferred source of identity. Loneliness is cool. Heroes hurt. Suffering is my super-power. I am Batman; I will rise again.

This self-narrative fits neatly within the framework of an ideology called Critical Race Theory (CRT), which portrays all human suffering as being due to oppressive social systems (victimization) and proposes aggressively proactive reforms through legal and social activism (heroism). Proponents of CRT seek to unearth, expose, and deconstruct what are seen to be false assumptions behind accepted socio-cultural norms that they deem to be oppressive. Although called a "theory," this is not just a matter of theoretical interest for the global majority. Identifying and acknowledging discrimination directly impacts "who has power, voice, and representation and who does not."[2]

An example of CRT might be if someone were to make the claim, "Abortion is wrong." CRT might respond: "That assumption comes out of a socially dominant white, conservative Western construct. We reject that: who are you to make that judgment call?" We can see another example in recent reactions to the Black Lives Matter movement, with

---

[2] Richard Delgado and Jean Stefancic, *Critical Race Theory: An Introduction* (New York, NY: New York University Press, 2001) 55.

some saying, "Black people are being selfish, overly-sensitive, unfair, unreasonable, and are aggressively contributing to moral and societal decay." CRT might respond: "That is the false assumption coming out of twelve generations of white, affluent European settlers who cannot see outside of their own bubble of safety and privilege." Point taken.

Critical Race Theory seeks to modify our post-Enlightenment fixation on empirical reason (objective data, logic) with an emphasis on *lived experience*. It teaches that what one feels (subjectivity) is as important as any other measurable (objective) reality. It questions whether there can be any real, measurable objective truth at all, since we are each shaped by, and therefore blind to, our own social biases. CRT might say, "My personal experience of *feeling* oppressed and undervalued carries more weight than my boss's assertion that this cannot be true, because our workplace has an equal rights protocol and a harassment officer in HR in place to prevent that."

As a tool for social reform, CRT has had immense merit for society in general. CRT teaches us to value a person's subjective experience and not dismiss the pain of anyone's trauma as being insignificant or unwarranted. It calls for people to become more empathetic and better listeners. It also calls for action. For Christians, CRT serves to remind us that we are here to do more than just share the gospel in word; we need to live the gospel through our actions. This means that the Church must do more than merely meeting needs (spiritual, social, emotional, physical) *when we become aware of them,* but that we should actually be initiating the search for those needs. Turn rocks over, dig deeper, lean into relationships. Rather than assume that someone is fine unless they say otherwise, we should initiate deeper conversations and probing queries all the time. "How are you? Are you really okay? Are we okay with each other? Is there something that I need to own, work on, apologize for, learn, help change?"

Critics ague that there is a growing culture of perpetual outrage associated with CRT. Yet the rampant rants of angry accusation on social media can also serve to challenge the Church to "turn the other cheek" on a whole new, radically uncomfortable level, and that is not a bad thing. The bar is being raised. This is particularly true for the North

American church, stereo-typically portrayed as white, Western, male, and middle-aged. True, we have not personally owned slaves, and to face the gale of pain unleashed by the Black Lives Matter movement is to feel accused, misjudged, even hated unfairly. To then answer with, "Your pain is real. Your story matters, you matter. I want to help; teach me how," requires a humility that quite frankly few of us possess. In all this, proponents of CRT can help the Church to grow up.

But there is also great danger. As oppressed individuals and groups are finally, and increasingly, given the voice and platform they deserve, there is an ironic and destructive side effect that CRT did not anticipate. Victims are now the role models for this generation. This would perhaps be a good thing, if the focus were on how they have overcome their circumstances and advocated for justice. But instead, there is an unexamined value emerging, the belief that one *must* suffer in order to have value. In other words, if you want to be a hero, you must first become a victim. With the heightened public exposure that comes through social media, there can even be a disturbing competitiveness that arises. This is being made even more acute by an increased focus on sub-categories of discrimination, leading to a hierarchy of victimhood in which individuals and groups compete for status based on who suffers the most.

Intersectionality, a now-popular term first coined decades ago by Kimberlé Crenshaw,[3] a leading scholar of CRT, adds a layer of complexity to this issue. Crenshaw identifies valid sub-genres of discrimination (being both Black and female, for example), which may be increasingly individualistic (being Black, female, poor, and disabled). This is a hot topic in academic and activist circles alike. On the plus side, intersectionality offers a more tailored approach to addressing the needs of marginalized individuals and avoids a one-size-fits-all solution to social reform. Each individual has a unique story, suffers uniquely, and must have their specific needs addressed. This approach decreases the sense of isolation that individuals who experience more than one

---

[3] Kimberlé Crenshaw, "Demarginalizing the Intersection of Race and Sex: A Black Feminist Critique of Antidiscrimination Doctrine, Feminist Theory and Antiracist Politics," University of Chicago Legal Forum, University of Chicago Law School, 1989.

category of oppression feel and can go a long way toward healing. But it can also backfire, big time.

There exists now a growing cynicism towards those who claim victimization, a cynicism provoked by what can seem like a growing competitiveness between micro-sub-genres of discrimination all vying for attention, making a mockery of what should be a valid and helpful social theory. Opportunists with a specific political agenda nurture outrage in order to rally supporters around their particular cause. The subsequent amplification of anger has, at least in the short-term, led to greater polarization and even violence. This creates an unsafe social arena in which the very people experiencing an intersection of specific modes of oppression may now be afraid to speak up.

Victimization is very real, but as a chosen, preferred identity, victimhood is self-defeating. Taking our primary identity in being victims ultimately only serves to fuel the fires of injustice. Paradigm-shaping theories like CRT can encourage us to hold up a reductionist meta-narrative of history, in which oppression is the main problem, and aggressive reform the only solution. In this scenario, utopia can never be reached, only an exchange of oppressive regimes. In contrast, Christianity holds up a meta-narrative in which *sin* is the main problem, and *Jesus* the only solution. Both ideologies advocate for social justice, but Christianity does so with the perspective that victims, heroes, and oppressors alike are all broken people in need of a Saviour.

When we feel out sync or insignificant, we can identify ourselves as victims. We start to feel marginalized—a state in which we feel alienated from everyone and everything. In short, we get stuck on the societal fringe. And therein lies a grave threat. For that fringe can become our Egypt, a place of temporary safe refuge that slowly becomes normative and familiar until, before we know it, we are content to be enslaved there. We cling to our comforts of bitterness, busyness, or bodily pleasures and convince ourselves that our prison is really quite pleasant, thank you very much. We find pockets of like-minded misfits, huddle together, and reinforce each other's bitterness against whatever common enemy we can blame for our feelings of marginalization. We form small colonies with those who share our grievances and call it community.

Our particular societal fringe begins to feel like home when, in reality, it is a refugee camp. One which, even when the opportunity is offered, we may refuse to leave. This was the case with the Hebrews in the days of Moses.

LET MY PEOPLE STAY

In the book of Exodus, Egypt illustrates the great irony of human nature. We cling to whatever has become familiar because familiarity makes us feel safe. The irony lies in the fact that the line between safety and slavery is a very fine one.

For close to three thousand years, the Egyptian empire was the dominant power of the ancient world. This advanced civilization offered both military protection and material benefits to all of its inhabitants, including slaves. For Jacob and his tribe, Egypt offered refuge from a severe drought-induced famine and a place where they could live and multiply so long as Joseph had favour with the governing pharaohs. These Hebrews were at first welcomed as honoured guests and given a lush region of their own in a land flowing with milk and honey. It was a little like staggering out of the desert, parched and near death, and finding yourself poolside at a luxury resort in Las Vegas.

Yearly flooding of the Nile deposited rich sediment that allowed huge variety of produce to grow. The Egyptian diet was a culinary dream come true: leeks, onions, garlic, cucumbers, lettuce, cabbages, radishes, grapes, figs, pomegranates, melons, and dates were available year-round. Fish were plentiful and easily obtained, breads and pastries were rich with olive oil, nuts, honey, and dates. The mild climate encouraged water sports, sunbathing (and Sun worshipping) scanty clothing, sumptuous dining, and both casual and creative sexuality. The Egyptian menu of gods was as extensive as their menu of foods. Pharaoh was considered a god, and other popular deities included Ra, the sun god; Hapi, the god of the Nile; Isis, the goddess of motherhood, magic, medicine, and peace; Osiris, the god of the afterlife; and a collection of animal gods, such as the cat and the crocodile. Egypt was certainly not boring.

Because they were able to keep themselves relatively autonomous in the land of Goshen, which had been granted to them during Joseph's lifetime, the Hebrews seemed as content to dwell there on the fringes of Egyptian culture as their hosts were to have them. This easy symbiosis continued for a couple of hundred years, long after the famine ended. The Hebrews grew comfortable and appeared to have no intention of moving out. Their temporary place of refuge had become their home. They no longer considered the words of their forefather Abraham concerning a destiny in some distant, inconvenient promised land. Why rock the boat? Then, in the midst of their complacency, the all-inclusive vacation suddenly turned into a death camp.

After Joseph's death, the Egyptians began to resent their freeloading guests and fear that they were becoming so numerous that they might pose a threat—either through open rebellion or through economic realities of hosting a people that held themselves apart from the religious and cultural mainstream of Egyptian society. A new ruling pharaoh decided to take action and enslave them (Exodus 1:9–11). The Bible uses words such as "bitter affliction," and "oppression" to describe the Israelites' lives at this time:

> *And the Egyptians made the children of Israel to serve with rigour: And they made their lives bitter with hard bondage, in mortar, and in brick, and in all manner of service in the field: all their service, wherein they made them serve, was with rigour.* (Exodus 1:13–14, KJV)

The Hebrew word for rigour, *perek*, means "harshness, severity, and cruelty." Midwives were commanded to kill any newborn Israelite boys, and soldiers went door-to-door to find young boys, impale them on their spears, and fling them into the Nile. Adult Hebrews were forced to make bricks from the mud left behind by the Nile, back-breaking work as they dug it out of the ground, moulded heavy bricks, and then carried them to a building site in brutally hot temperatures. The suffering was unimaginable. And, apparently, necessary.

When we cling to an identity that has brought us comfort in the past, it takes intolerable pain to make us let it go. God was determined to break the stronghold of the Hebrews's addiction to a shallow identity and a meaningless life. Egypt was not their destiny, and God would not let them stay there. He painfully weans them later in Exodus, when Pharaoh's heart is alternately hardened by Pharaoh himself (Exodus 8:15; 8:32; 9:34) and then by God's own hand (Exodus 7:3, 13; 9:12; 10:1, 20, 27; 11:10; 14:4, 8). There is a certain ruthlessness about God's resolve to rescue his people from the prison cell which they had come to furnish and regard with such fondness.

The process of freeing the Hebrews was not accomplished in a short time. It took more than departing from Goshen or parting the Red Sea. For the next forty years, God's people whimpered and clutched the broken chains of their bondage to their bosom whenever the pace of change and challenge frightened them. A lack of water in the wilderness lead them to regret their exodus, hunger lead to lament over the plentiful pots of meat they had left behind, and years of manna made the miraculous seem mundane. Faced with the reality of war against the Canaanites, they begged to to go back to the land of their misery (Numbers 14:1–4). Better to be slave with a full belly than to come against Canaanite giants with sharpened swords.

Change is not easy. Even when that change is clearly for the better, we hold on to what is routine, what is familiar. We choose life on the fringe and resist freedom.

LIFE ON THE FRINGE

Misfits both want, and do not want, to belong. Like the Hebrew slaves, we both want, and do not want, to be free. We fear the unfamiliar, we worry that we will lose ourselves, lose whatever tenuous identity we have managed to cobble together over the years. We so fear losing our unique qualities that we search out those less admirable qualities in others so that we might, in their company, assure ourselves that we're a special or even superior minority. We start clubs and Facebook rants and write anti-books for the sole purpose of proving others wrong. We refuse to join anything. Teams will swallow us alive. We fear becoming another faceless, homogeneous unit within the proverbial *melting pot.*[4] Assimilation is a terrifying prospect, for it implies invisibility. And, while the segregated autonomy of our affinity sub-group may be more appealing, it is also terrifying, for it presents the claustrophobic prospect of being forced to associate only with those who are Just Like Me.

We are stuck on the fringe, both wanting and not wanting to be there. Those who do not share our struggles can be perplexed and encourage us to join a club or support group to meet our specific areas of social dysfunction or standing. Some genuinely want to help and want us to have friends. Others nudge us towards groups of people who share our particular struggles, perhaps because it's too much work to befriend us themselves. Even our education and health care systems routinely send those on the societal fringes to affinity-based, mono-generational sub-groups. Yet it often backfires.

At first, encouraging someone to join an affinity group may seem like an obvious step towards social integration, and indeed it may be helpful at the start. Consider, for example, sending an alcoholic uncle to join Alcoholics Anonymous, sending an autistic child to a special needs class, sending a newly diagnosed diabetic to a support group to learn about how to cope with the disease, and so on. Affinity groups can be invaluable stepping stones toward integration and belonging. But they can also become a prison. Once part of the club, it may be difficult to escape. One close friend of mine, whom I will call Lisa, tells of her experience with an affinity group.

***

I am an older single woman who is often lonely, and so I joined a support group for other women in the same situation. Our

---

[4] In *Multiculturalism and Politics of Recognition* (Princeton University Press; 1992), Mark Taylor warns that we do others a great disservice when we do not endeavour to discover the unique identity of each individual or cultural group, and acknowledge their distinctiveness from everyone else. He writes, "With Western tendencies towards assimilation of minority groups the ensuing 'non-recognition or misrecognition' can inflict harm, can be a form of oppression, imprisoning someone in a false, distorted, and reduced mode of being" (25).

meetings were helpful at first, and it comforted me to know that my emotions and experiences were not abnormal. Online chats lead to the formation of a private social media group. Soon, the internet reflected its uncanny awareness, with marketing agencies monitoring our search engines and sending customized pop-up ads to catch our fancy. Our group signed up for a single's cruise, and then we began to vacation together.

Our conversations were more and more about the shared problems that we were facing—loneliness, bitterness about men. Before long, I realized that I was actually getting more and more angry and hard, and our gossip and complaining was actually alienating us more from others, not bringing us into healthy community at all! I stepped back and looked at myself, at us, and thought, "What man would ever want to approach me? No wonder I'm alone!"

***

Society has a tendency to deal with those on the fringes by labelling, sorting, and filing us all. Hundreds of new Facebook target-groups are created daily, inviting followers to join based on their political ideology, ethnicity, gender inclination, moral outrage, and more. We are categorized—and grouped accordingly—by our personal preferences, achievements, perceived dysfunctions, and needs. This is meant to create a sense of belonging, of being in community. But in fact, it is a false community, a mono-community, and such segregation makes our loneliness far worse. Kenneth Cragg was an Anglican bishop and who worked extensively in Christian–Muslim relations and became Assistant Bishop of Jerusalem in 1969. He says:

> We disentangle misunderstandings. We reaffirm positions. We maintain politeness. We even repent. What then? For the most part, we stay in our positions, sometimes failing to take in what the other means. Response sometimes reveals that we are not responding.... The issues are profound. They are about the basic

questions of the human situation. This means that in the hearing and the giving of witness in dialogue there is pain. Perhaps we mutually fear the pain.[5]

Loneliness and fear are always intensified for those who come from a different background, and it is natural to want to avoid that pain. But is it healthy? Avoiding those who are different seems to be our default setting.

The modern Church is not much different, advocating for affinity groups to build community and a sense of belonging. When churches create affinity groups, congregants are invited to separate themselves according to gender, age, marital status, health, hobbies, talents, and troubles. This neat compartmentalization may reflect the well-meaning intentions of godly caring pastors who are eager to slot us into spaces where we may belong. Or, it could also be a convenient way to avoid awkward social clashes. Ideally, church affinity groups allow people the most personal comfort presumably so that they can create lasting friendships. But, ironically, affinity groups also contribute to the formation of individualistic mono-cultures which are often rife with even greater loneliness for all concerned.

Let me point out here that Western individualism, however it may influence global theologies, is not, in fact, the global norm. On any given Sunday, average North American Christians attend the church which best fits with their personal preferences. They gather with fellow believers who are, for the most part, just like them, to worship, pray, hear the Word of God, and engage with others. These basic elements comprise our Western understanding of the function of an *ecclesia*, the Greek word used to describe a *gathering* of the early Christians. To varying degrees, these activities also occur in mid-week small group meetings, and it is only here that most Western Christians might be forced to encounter and adapt to the uncomfortable differences in theology, ethics, values, and personalities of their peers. Yet it is within these uncomfortable situations that spiritual formation best occurs.

---

[5] Quoted in David W. Shenk and Badru Kateregga, *A Muslim and a Christian in Dialogue* (Harrisonburg, VA: Herald Press, 1997) 14–18.

The New Testament Church gatherings were also small, probably thirty or so members on average. However, the only commonality that might be present—aside from faith in Jesus—would be that the gatherings were comprised of those who belonged to the same household or guild. These small gatherings would not have considered themselves as the more personal, relational aspect of a larger Church (as we consider our mid-week meetings to be), but rather were the *only* "church" that early Christians knew. Both the New Testament Church and the gatherings encouraged during the Reformation were organic, geographically local, frequently biologically related, yet necessarily diverse. Jewish households of the day included extended family units, slaves, employees, business associates or clients, and "adopted" members who had been accepted into the family for various reasons. Converting to Christianity was often a corporate affair, and so subsequent church gatherings centred on this basic social unit. In short, they bore little resemblance to the modern mono-generational, small groups of today's Western Church.

It is a peculiarly Western assumption that the spiritual growth of individuals best occurs in an affinity group, rather than within the diversity of one's geographic locale. The global church reality is that few Majority World cultures enjoy the luxury of being able to shop around for a comfortable ecclesial "fit." In remote regions of rural Burundi, the local church community often consists of those who are within walking distance (by that I mean miles, not blocks) of the appointed Baobab tree where social gatherings occur. These believers may have little in common with one another in terms of social constructs or personal interests. They are drawn together because of their geographical proximity to one another, and their faith in Jesus.

Despite the fact that Christian churches insist that we are the family of God, our vastly different interpretations of that concept inevitably lead to frustration. We can be disappointed when we are limited to affinity-based community, especially when we only focus on ourselves and the common issues of those in the group. Affinity groups are helpful in the short-term for those looking for immediate connections. However, in the long haul, divorcees do not wish to only socialize with other divorcees, nor do seniors want to only meet with other seniors, recovering alcoholics with other recovering alcoholics, etc. Community without diversity is not community at all.

The dispersion at the Tower of Babel not only dissipated a potential global rebellion, it created a healthy, vital diversity that requires us to wrestle with our differences. It is a sign of our fear, pride, and brokenness when we gravitate towards affinity groups that limit our relational experience. We seek the easiest route, we avoid the challenges of change, and we flinch from tension and conflict. The Church may inadvertently accommodate our fear by supplying an endless array of shopping options so that we find the others who are most like ourselves, replacing the "us" of diverse biblical community with the artificial construct of a bigger "me." For those already experiencing isolation and loneliness, it is decidedly unhelpful to limit the social circle to only other isolated or lonely peers. We all want friends, but we don't benefit from exclusively homogeneous communities, even supposing such a community could be found.

Transitioning to diverse community is threatening. We fear the potential loss of Self that comes from integration as much as we fear being alone or trapped in affinity groups with those who merely mirror our own struggles. Consider the plight of new immigrants and their children. Fear can drive them in one of two directions: either they completely renounce the majority values of their existing affinity group altogether (not uncommon with second generation immigrants and MK's who reject their parent's faith and traditions) and form a new group, or they blindly cling to whatever is most familiar and avoid integration with anyone who is different (as with some first generation immigrants). These reactions fracture society further by widening the rift between economic classes, religious groups, and generations. Children of new immigrants, for example, may begin to associate their parents' values with outdated ideological, religious, or ethnic traditions. The second generation may feel the need to integrate into a new culture and renounce their family altogether, leaving little else to fill the gap in their identity than rabid materialism or the superior disdain projected by the media and reflected by their peers.

Identity crisis is not only painful; it can become dangerous. When our sense of Self is disrupted, one of two things can occur. We may experience an alarming increase in aggression and hostility or, conversely, helpless passivity. When identity is threatened or taken away from us, we may seek to re-establish it through passively surrendering, submerging our autonomy, or even accepting abuse. Miroslav Volf addresses this in his book, *A Spacious Heart: Essays on Identity and Belonging*. He writes:

> The desire for identity could also explain why so many people let themselves be sinned against so passively—why they let themselves be excluded. It is not because they do not have the will to be themselves, but because one can satisfy that will by surrendering to the other.... Their problem is a paradoxical exclusion of their own self from the will to be oneself (what in feminist theology is called the "diffusion of the self").... Like Cain, we then become ready to kill the otherness of the other.[6]

The stress of threatened and deconstructed identity experienced by new immigrants and their children is appalling. It can cause a wide scope of reactions: one day adopting an identity of helpless victimization, another day angrily lashing out. They may have an intense desire to submerge all cultural distinctions, rejecting the values of any previous cultural or religious context altogether, in order to feel accepted. They may feel a defiant, militant desire to have their own cultural distinctions acknowledged as being superior. Or they may feel both impulses at the same time. Emotional paralysis can set in. Setting goals and making decisions can become an overwhelming, infuriating task. Friends and extended family may become confused, not knowing how to help. What is most needed? Rescue, admiration, empowerment, vindication, or a listening ear? Friends my offer a helpful hand, only to be slapped away. Stress can easily reach critical levels, with outbreaks of violence, alcoholism, abuse, teenage rebellion, and divorce common among new immigrant families.

The danger is very real for all of us who struggle with this degree of identity crisis. We are capable of extreme reactions and harmful acts to

---

[6] Judith M. Gundry-Volf and Miroslav Volf, *A Spacious Heart: Essays on Identity and Belonging* (Harrisburg, PA: Trinity Press International, 1997) 54–55.

ourselves and others. Considering all of this, perhaps the story of Moses is hardly surprising. He was destined to be a misfit from the day he was conceived.

PRINCE OF EGYPT

There were enough elements surrounding Moses's gestation, birth, and early years to doom him to a life of confusion, conflicting loyalties, anger, and frustration. Adoption by an Egyptian oppressor would certainly have added to the stress, with both sets of parents—Hebrew slaves on the one hand, and Egyptian royalty on the other—projecting their own desires on him and assigning roles to him. It was a perfect recipe for an identity crisis, as there was a good chance Moses would be a disappointment to one or both of his mothers. Their expectations were, after all, rather high. His biological parents knew that he was *"no ordinary child"* (Hebrews 11:23), perhaps foreseeing his role as the deliverer of the Hebrews, and his adoptive mother, the daughter of Pharaoh, likely had a distinguished military career in mind for his future. Neither could have foreseen him becoming a murderer and an outcast.

Raised in a palace, Moses would have been groomed for a high-ranking military position within a liberal society that tolerated, even encouraged, ethnic diversity in professional roles. The historian Josephus writes, in *The Antiquities of the Jews,* of Moses as having risen to the rank of general in the Egyptian army, and this is certainly not an unlikely scenario. If his royal family were not directly in the line of succession, Moses would have been trained for a career in the diplomatic corps as a military leader of high rank.[7] The children of royalty and favoured officials were entrusted to a royal tutor and taught not just basic reading and writing skills, but the hieratic shorthand of hieroglyphic script, as well as Babylonian cuneiform script, these being the languages of diplomacy in the ancient Near East. Moses would also have been privy to the vast wealth of texts in the royal archives and led to study mathematics and astronomy. This Hebrew foster child would have received the best education available in the ancient world.

---

[7] Joann Fletcher, *Chronicle of a Pharaoh: The Intimate Life of Amenhotep III* (New York, NY: Oxford University Press, 2000) 24–27.

Because of this, we can assume that Moses was all too keenly aware of the critical conflict of interests, and the political and moral dilemma he was in, making his rank and privilege seem ironic and meaningless. For his Egyptian benefactors were in fact bullies, and there came a day when he could no longer stand idly by and allow the abuse of his brethren to continue.

A VIOLENT CLASH OF ROLES

We might imagine Moses as a rather conflicted individual when he was forty years of age. Without a doubt he was greatly loved by his birth parents, and likely strongly counselled by Amram and Jochebed, his mother and Levite father, against adopting the values of their Egyptian oppressors. Yet, he had been adopted as an Egyptian prince. It seems inevitable that Moses would long to identify himself with a single cultural group. But which group? His biological parents saw him as destined for greatness. His adoptive family may have seen him as likewise destined for greatness, but of a different sort, perhaps as a future dignitary in Egypt. All of this may have played into how Moses perceived himself when, one fateful day, his roles clashed in a single act of violence. In Exodus 2:11–12 we read:

> *One day, after Moses had grown up, he went out to where his own people were and watched them at their hard labor. He saw an Egyptian beating a Hebrew, one of his own people. Looking this way and that and seeing no one, he killed the Egyptian and hid him in the sand.*

Years of identity crisis had torn his heart in two, alternately compelling him to embrace his Hebrew roots and honour his royal Egyptian upbringing. Moses finally came to a breaking point. He broke out of the mould into which he had been crammed since infancy. By murdering the Egyptian soldier, he vented decades of pent-up grief, frustrated longing, and anger at social injustice. Here was a man who desperately wanted to belong, to be accepted, and to be allowed to identify with the Hebrew brethren from whom he felt constantly, subtly, maddeningly estranged. Moses chose to align himself definitively with an abused Hebrew and kill an Egyptian soldier. The book of Hebrews tells us that he was aware of his actions:

> *By faith Moses, when he had grown up, refused to be known as the son of Pharaoh's daughter. He chose to be mistreated along with the people of God rather than to enjoy the fleeting pleasures of sin. He regarded disgrace for the sake of Christ as of greater value than the treasures of Egypt, because he was looking ahead to his reward. By faith he left Egypt, not fearing the king's anger; he persevered because he saw him who is invisible.* (11:24–27)

Moses knew full well that he was rejecting his chance to rule in Egypt. Had he aligned himself with Egypt, he would likely have been given a military commission, with authority to rule its vassals, including the Hebrews. But he declined the opportunity to rule over the Hebrews because he wanted to be *one of them*. Significantly, Moses did not take advantage of his rank and position that day and simply order the Egyptian soldier to stop beating the Hebrew slave. He might have endeavoured to use his own authority as an Egyptian noble to oppose the unjust oppression of his own people, but he did not. Despite the definitive action of killing an oppressor, Moses did not act with bold confidence.

By defending the slave, Moses openly aligned himself with the Hebrews, yet he didn't follow it up with a strident declaration of his allegiance with them. He didn't attempt to start an insurgency, defying the Egyptian oppressors. And, while this violent act was a spontaneous outburst of outrage, Moses took the time to look around and make sure no other Egyptians were watching. He knew what he was doing was wrong. The killing was not a bold, decisive act in support of his Hebrew heritage. Rather, it was covert, secret. Why?

Moses may have wanted to cast his lot wholly with his people, but he was still pulled between the two cultures in which he was raised. His actions were extreme, but showed the tension of indecision. Even as he rejected one identity in favour of the other, Moses was afraid. He wasn't ready to be publicly defiant, not ready to reject his adoptive parentage outright, not ready to start a formal rebellion and lead a revolt among the Hebrew slaves. Though he was rejecting one identity, he wasn't yet fully asserting another. Moses may have had dreams of being a welcomed, lauded hero and delivering his Hebrew brethren, but he clearly wasn't prepared to take a definitive stand against Egypt that day, or the next.

Moses was still of two minds, not wanting to burn his bridges with Egypt, yet determined to identify with the Hebrews. Determined to be one of them. Determined to find acceptance and to finally fit in. It didn't work.

WHO MADE YOU JUDGE?

As Moses feared, the murder was witnessed, although not by any Egyptians. The next day, Moses's tentative identification as a fellow Hebrew was rejected. Seeing two Hebrew slaves fighting with each other, he dared to intervene, only to be sharply rebuffed for his audacity. How dare he presume to be one of them, much less their leader!

> *The next day he went out and saw two Hebrews fighting. He asked the one in the wrong, "Why are you hitting your fellow Hebrew?" The man said, "Who made you ruler and judge over us? Are you thinking of killing me as you killed the Egyptian?" Then Moses was afraid and thought, "What I did must have become known."* (Exodus 2:13–14)

This was not the warm welcome or affirmation of who Moses may have thought (or hoped) himself to be. On the contrary, the very ones with whom Moses sought to identify himself were now a threat to him. There is resentment and aggression in the rebuke: "Who made you ruler and judge over us? Are you going to kill me as you killed the Egyptian?" Instead of being seen as a deliverer, Moses was sneered at by those that he tried to help. And retreat was not an option. His Egyptian family, who had cared for him his whole life, now sought to kill him. Rejected by all, every aspect of Moses's identity shattered that day.

When Moses lost his role-based identities, he lost everything he had. Yet somehow, he left Egypt with a knowledge that he had, that day, broken free from the roles that held him captive. Regardless of the contempt he received from his fellow Hebrews, Moses knew that he had made the right choice to align himself with God's people. As he left Egypt behind, he perhaps also left behind some of his confusion. It was no longer relevant if he was seen as an Egyptian or Hebrew. He now belonged to no one, except perhaps to God. Yet it was still a bitter event, and his long exile in Midian took its toll on his fragile sense of Self. There, he came to a place of brokenness, the realization that he was helpless, in his own strength, to ever become the person that God called him to be. It was only when he reached that place of utter dependency and humility that God stepped in and turned his life upside down. Like Moses, perhaps we need to be homeless in spirit before we can understand God's plan for our lives.

As Christ followers, we are called to be "in" but not "of" this world, called to embrace the rootless and restless aspects of our lives. We are meant to be out of sync, citizens of another realm living in healthy cross-cultural tension here on planet Earth as ambassadors to the nations. And so, those who wrestle most with their sense of identity may, in fact, be the very ones who have been sent by God to disturb the rest of us with a much-needed, divine discontent. How do we do this? Before we can discern the "what" of our calling, we must identify *to whom* we have been sent.

ON BEING SENT

Jorge was polite, but guarded, with the other graduate students, carefully reading them for social cues. I assumed it was a language issue; English was, after all, not his native tongue, as he had been born in Argentina to Taiwanese parents before immigrating to Canada. As the cohort concluded its group discussion we headed back to the collegium for coffee. There, I noticed a Spanish-speaking colleague approach Jorge and engage him in conversation. The change in his demeanour was startling.

Cracking jokes and gesticulating expressively, Jorge was captivating. When an older Asian student suddenly called out to him, however, he immediately inclined his head and bowed slightly.

The ensuing conversation was stiff, formal, with little or no eye contact; in all, an appropriately respectful Asian response to being addressed by an elder.

Later, Jorge and I chatted about what I had observed.

"Seriously!" I laughed. "That's some kind of personality syndrome you have! So, who on Earth are you, really?"

Jorge shook his head at my confusion. "I honestly don't know," he confessed ruefully. "I guess it depends on where I am sent."

***

Followers of the incarnate God are called to bridge the abyss. Like Jesus, Christians are called to identify with the people to whom we have been sent. It isn't meant to be easy. Whatever the comfortable, familiar trappings of our lives might be, we are called to set them aside for the sake of entering into the strangeness of some one else's context. We will feel an inevitable sense of anxiety and loss as we do this, but God's intervention into our world through Jesus assures us that we are invited to be part of a culture that is bigger, divine, and eternal: the Kingdom of God. In order to extend this kingdom, we must reach the lost. But before we can reach them, it is helpful to know who they are. To whom, exactly, have we each been sent?

Jesus was able to engage and challenge the cultures of the day because he understood them intimately; in his incarnation, he knew that he was *sent* to identify with the Hebrews. He put off the divine, clothing himself instead in uncomfortable, unclean, and unfamiliar human flesh. He was circumcised, learned to speak the local languages, ate ethnic food, and laboured at a socially acceptable trade. He agreed to be baptized—a cultural norm of the times—in spite of the fact that he was sinless. In so doing, Jesus stood in solidarity with humanity, praying the kinds of prayers spoken by Daniel (9:4–19), Ezra (9:6–15), and Nehemiah (1:5–11) in identification with their people.

Jesus became one with those to whom he was sent without losing sight of his mission. He identified with them *so that* he might better reach them. He adapted himself to Jewish temple worship and synagogue teaching practices so that he might, with a quote from Isaiah, herald his ministry on Earth and usher in the Kingdom of God. He chose the well-known role of a wandering rabbi, solidifying his message of salvation with culturally contextual literary devices and allegories *so that* his stories might touch the hearts the common people Galilee. Moreover, Jesus made friends, even though he didn't need to in order to communicate his message and accomplish his redemptive purposes, *so that* we might see his heart and know that we were seeing the Father.

For over three years, the Messiah lived and travelled with the apostles, sharing meals, money, miracles, and misery. Through it all, he remained imminently accessible to his friends in every way. Jesus was never aloof or emotionally self-protective with them. On the contrary, he invited them—not once, but three times—to witness and participate in the vulnerability of his suffering at Gethsemane. In every possible way, Jesus embraced his humanness, for he had given up everything in order to identify with those to whom he was sent. This included even his very life, for ultimately, a truly incarnational mission requires death, whether literal or figurative.

"Death to Self" may sound romantic, even noble, but it is still death. We read in Mark 8:34–35:

> *Then [Jesus] called the crowd to him along with his disciples and said: 'Whoever wants to be my disciple must deny themselves and take up their cross and follow me. For whoever wants to save their life will lose it, but whoever loses their life for me and for the gospel will save it.*

The word used here for "life" is *psuché*, meaning "the very essence of one's being." God surrendered the divine essence of his being to become human, that he might reach all humanity. In the sent-ness of his incarnation, Christ was the perfect missionary, who *"loved not [his life], even unto death"* (Revelations 12:11, ESV). It is in within this context that the Word becomes flesh, with the messengers themselves becoming part of the community and culture they are endeavouring to reach. It is a clear, biblical ideal that few would argue against. Many of us, however, find ourselves being sent to those with whom we have very little in common and question whether God really knows what he's doing. It's hardest to live sacrificially among those who we don't understand, and who don't understand us. David Livermore describes this kind of sacrificial living as a "messy, challenging process," which ultimately it reflects "God, the Holy Other... [who] reaches across every chasm of difference and meets us where we are."[8] We cannot be sent unless we are willing to leave home first. The stark abruptness of this kind of cultural transition can be overwhelming, even if the ones to whom we are sent appear, on the surface, to be like us in many ways.

Don't believe me? Try changing churches.

PLAY NICE, DEAR[9]

The greeter's eyes slid past to the elderly gentleman behind me, even as she extended her hand to bid me a bright and cheery "Good Morning!" The morning had little to say for itself in the face of such determined perkiness, I thought to myself.

Shaking hands, I was startled by the unexpected traction; firmly but kindly I was drawn across the Threshold of Indecision into the Chamber of Commitment, AKA, the church foyer. There was a brief moment of panic as I felt my fingers encased in an iron grip of friendliness, but it was too late to change my mind, and obviously futile to attempt to break loose. Crossing said threshold meant entering the holy hullaballoo beyond; was I really ready for that?

I lurched clumsily when my hand was suddenly released. The teeming crowd of happy, shiny, utterly unfamiliar faces was overwhelming. I was new. I was lost. I was terrified. I was also being gently prodded from behind by the greeter, a reminder that I was holding up the line, breaking the flow. Where was the next processing point? I had been successfully greeted; it was time to be "ushed."

The usher, an exemplar of politesse, wore a broad and steady smile even as his eyes darted with near-imperceptible rapidity over

---

[8] David A. Livermore, *Cultural Intelligence: Improving Your CQ to Engage Our Multi-Cultural World* (Grand Rapids, MI: Baker Academic Press, 2009) 256.

[9] This section is modified from my article "Menno-Nice," originally published in the July 2009 issue of the *MB Herald*.

*my face and attire. He creased his brow slightly, perhaps trying
to place my origins. Who was I? Was I a Thiessen, or Friesen, or
Enns (Oh my)? None of the above, thank you very much; my people
hailed from the Orkneys in Northern Scotland. Small, dark, wiry,
covered in blue tattoos, and prone to run naked and shrieking into
battle. Couldn't he tell?*

*Echoes of my own mother's voice rose up to haunt me. "Play
nicely with the other children, dear," she would say. My current
levels of adrenaline were definitely not on board with that. I was
under-dressed, over-stimulated, and frantic in the grip of some
ecclesial identity crisis.*

Where do I go? What do I do? How do I fit?

What on Earth am I doing here?!?

***

We were astounded by the grace extended to our family during the
difficult months as we transitioned to a new church. The first few weeks
were the hardest to navigate, but once the congregation recognized us as
"newbies," they lost no time trying to make us feel welcome, accepted,
valued, and useful. Staff and lay leadership were effusive and affirming.
Everyone was So Darned Nice. It was a little surreal, actually. Could
that many people really be that nice? I poked. No one poked back. Had
generations of in-breeding altered the genetic code? My Pictish blood
recoiled. How could I interact with such nice people?

My husband and I had just buried a father, a church, and a dog. I
missed the warmth of the Mexican culture that had been my home for
most of my youth. Our teenage son was in an ugly phase of rebellion.
We had lost a house, most of our savings, and all of our confidence. We
were living through a particularly bad set of country western lyrics and
no longer knew who we were or where we belonged. We were angry,
cynical, and suspicious of everyone, including God. We were, in fact,
not at all nice. How could we ever hope to find a new identity here?
What if we were the only misfits in the entire church?

MR. POTATO HEAD

The reality was that our church was like any other microcosm of diverse humanity, and we did eventually find others with whom we "fit." Yet, although we formed deep and lasting friendships over the years, neither we nor our children ever lost the slightly hunted, haunted demeanour of those living on the fringe. During the worst of it, the metaphor of the Church as being the Body of Christ offered little condolence for our social awkwardness. There were hands and feet and other useful organs, and then there were people like us, a double-jointed sixth toe, perhaps. A bit odd, certainly harder to find shoes for. Were we still a valid part of the Body? I recalled the extra bits and pieces that came in the box for Mr. Potato Head, a well-loved toy from my own childhood. Would we, along with those oddly-shaped lips that even a potato would not deign to wear, find ourselves stuck in a box on some dusty shelf?

Admittedly, there were certain advantages to having a skewed, off-beat aspect to our family. For one, it enabled us to quickly spot others who, like us, perched precariously on the edge of the social fringe, in danger of ditching church altogether. Fully empathetic with their plights, we became skilled at connecting other misfits to the mainstream church, endeavouring to make the daunting prospect of fellowship among the fit and functional seem a little more attainable. Interestingly, over the years, we noticed that those with whom we connected best seemed to fit into consistent categories: current and ex-missionaries, migrants and new immigrants, and those who categorized themselves as dysfunctional because of physiological, mental, or emotional challenges. Missionaries, migrants, and misfits. What on Earth did we all have in common, and why? Had we been sent to them, or had we all, as a group of oddballs, been sent to disturb the "normality" of the mainstream church? And, if so, did we really want that assignment?

It was difficult for us to embrace our sent-ness as a primary identity when we had a chip on our shoulders the size of a small Mid-Western state. We were in a full-fledged identity crisis, unsure of who we were being called to become, or whether we really wanted to co-operate at all. But it seemed that before we could know who we were, we had first to firmly establish who we were *not*. My sensitive MK/PK husband did not to fit with the plaid-shirted hockey enthusiasts. My daughter had no desire to do a rotation in the church nursery. I cringed at the thought of quilting clubs and crafts. We all tried on a variety of hats, as it were, and a few years of trial and error helped clarify our identity through the process of elimination.

Before we can embrace a new, God-given identity, we must divest ourselves of false identities, those definitions of self that come from sources other than God. As we will see, Moses faced this challenge and was not always successful in shrugging off the identities that he had adopted for himself, or had placed upon him by others.

What exactly are the sources of false identity, and why do they grip us so powerfully?

CHAPTER THREE
Who Am I Not?

ROLES, RELATIONSHIPS, AND SELF-REALIZATION

As far as ice-breakers went, it was not too painful. This was our first meeting as a mission team, and we were given precisely one minute in which, through pithy conversation and astute questioning, we were to introduce ourselves to each member of the team. Within seconds, I could feel my frustration rise.

Other teammates had asked me the questions "Where were you born? How long have you been married? How many children do you have? What are your hobbies?" a total of four times, and I was losing whatever fragile grip I had upon my impulse control. We were barely breaking the surface here. Before stranger number five could ask the same questions, I snapped.

"My name is Nikki. I am socially awkward, prefer solitude and silence whenever possible, but am prone to sporadic bouts of relational intensity. I need everyone around me to feel as uncomfortable as I feel, so cross-cultural missions suit me just fine. I am border-line OCD, so I get a lot done fast, but when I am being really creative, I sometimes lose the ability to swallow. I hate the colour beige, I play Scrabble for money, and I have seriously asked God for the gift of astral travel. I want you to like me, but I

worry that you will be put off, or worse, impressed, or worse still, indifferent."

I paused and sat back, checking the timer. "And you?"

***

Each generation faces a degree of identity crisis at some point, whether that be the post-war boomer in mid life, the twenty-first-century daughter of feminism ashamed to admit her fondness for domesticity, or the boomerang child who is no longer able to return to his parents' home, and is reluctantly facing the financial responsibility of adulthood. The simplicity of childhood is all too soon challenged by the frightening variety of options that demand a certainty of direction that few adolescents possess. We are told that we should have a firm sense of Self in order to wade through the fog of our own identity crises. But where does that conviction of identity come from? How can we be sure we're defining ourselves correctly and not falling prey to prideful self-deception, the defeatist voices of our own past, or the labels of the world?

The uncertainty is heightened by the knowledge that, as followers of Christ, we are called to be leaders in this world, setting a confident pace and direction for others, assured of our salvation, convinced of our calling, bold in our actions. Few of us ever reach this level of conviction. Instead, we remain largely ambivalent about our divine purpose outside of a general social conscience that guides our actions and a fuzzy "groupthink" that dictates our morality, recreational boundaries, and choice of clothing and hairstyles. Finding out "who we are" ceases to be a compelling priority so long as we have some way to adapt and blend into whatever surrounds us. We care more about "fitting in" with the crowd than about "fitting into" God's plan for our lives. It's a small wonder that the world we have been sent to transform becomes, instead, the voice that defines us. In the world, we are defined according to what can be measured: the concrete, tangible parameters of career, social status, family, and recreational preferences. Rather than allow God to define us according to eternal standards, we allow the definitions of Roles, Relationships, and Self-realization to label and limit us.

ROLES: I AM WHAT I DO

The world often defines us by the roles thrust upon us. There is barely time to reflect upon our calling or dreams when we have to deal with the hectic pace of life, and so we inevitably resort to a definition of self that concedes, "I am what I do." When we meet someone new, most of us ask, "What do you do?" and then offer our career or occupation in return. This has been a predominant means of evaluating people since the Industrial Revolution, when productivity became the driving force behind society.

Post-WWII job security anchored itself in mass manufacturing, and the resulting consumerism created a society in which production exceeded actual needs, changing us from a "needs-based" to a "wants-based" economy. This system perpetuates dissatisfaction in every possible way. The very process of satisfying our desires creates even more desire. In such a system, our desires can never be truly satisfied.

Ironically, the advent of a wants-based society brought an emphasis on self-actualization with it. As identity became intrinsically entwined with the potential to achieve, the goal of achievement was constantly reassessed by the fluctuating whimsy of affluent consumers. As David Livermore attests, Western culture is "extremely skewed toward the 'doing' side of the continuum. Tasks, accomplishments, and efficiency are the standards for success..."[10] In such a context, it is impossible to ever "arrive" at the point of success. As the finish line keeps moving, our ambition and anxiety increase, reaching a crisis when we can't meet our goals because we feel inadequate, or because the economy sets higher and higher standards for productivity and then discards those who can't make their quota.

A SHABBY REALITY

My spouse, a "tekkie" by education, trade, and inclination, has faced multiple bouts of unemployment in the course of our (thus far) thirty-five years of marriage. Abandoning a career path in favour of a missional lifestyle in our early years took its toll on our finances and security. Each lay-off brought another crisis of identity and self-worth. At first,

---

[10] Livermore, *Cultural Intelligence*, 225.

we would go through a week or two of shock, and the associated lack of proactive thought or action as we "processed" the disaster. Then we would spring into a flurry of activity: networking, identifying job-sites, re-working resumes, and re-assessing the household budget. To our credit, God did feature in our fluster, and we would frequently stop for tea and prayer. At these times, we experienced near-euphoria in the crisis, a kind of romance in the catastrophe that loomed. The euphoria normally ended by the third month. Life would become a shabby reality of bills, bad credit, and black holes into which resumes and applications were sent, never to be seen or heard from again. We were overwhelmed with regret at ever having gone into the mission field at all.

The stress took its toll. We avoided social events, cringing at the possibility of facing the question: "And what do *you* do?" Normal life was put on hold. There were no extra-curricular activities for the children, no date nights, no enjoying a guilt-free sleep-in on Saturday mornings. Even daily devotions became a ritual of self-recrimination and desperate pleading. Whatever else God might have said during that time, we were unlikely to pause long enough to ask or listen. I watched my spouse's self-esteem plummet, and his irritation and anger grow. Our children avoided this grumpy stranger, put off by the undercurrent of inarticulate fear.

One cannot underestimate the blow that unemployment deals to self-esteem. Unemployment becomes a double crisis of financial duress and self-blame, with discouraged job-seekers losing momentum and confidence. In his book, *Flawed System/Flawed Self*, Ofer Sharone writes:

> ...American job-seekers [are] highly vulnerable to self-blame. This turns unemployment into a double crisis: in addition to the financial crisis of wondering how one will keep paying the bills and not lose one's home, there is the personal crisis of wondering, "What's wrong with me?"....These effects have consequences for society as well as for individuals.[11]

---

[11] Ofer Sharone, *Flawed System/Flawed Self: Job Searching and Unemployment Experiences* (Chicago, IL: University of Chicago Press, 2014) 2.

Sharone's observations are particularly true of Western cultures, which value the presentation of personality over resume, and value hard (technical) skills over the soft skills of empathy, persuasion, or creativity. Where once work was viewed as a human duty and source of social contribution, rising inflation and an ever-increasing materialistic world-view have transformed work into simply a means of living, a necessary activity. When we are less personally and emotionally invested in our careers, our job satisfaction lowers as well, creating an environment in which our self-worth is based almost entirely on the bottom line. And, when we lose our income, we have fewer social and relational props to prevent a sense of utter failure. Unemployment results in a vicious cycle of isolation and depression.

When we can't define our self-worth through our roles, the spiralling erosion of self-esteem can be brutal. When we don't feel like we're fulfilling our roles, or when our roles are in conflict, the result can be a kind of confused, emotional paralysis. Perhaps you have experienced this.

Moses did. But first he had to go through a significant time of growing in self-awareness. It takes some serious self-examination to get, as they say, "woke." My husband and I had, painfully, some help along the way.

GAME CHANGERS

My husband's last bout of unemployment occurred when we were both in our fifties. We were devastated. It's one thing to face starting over in the prime of life, but we had little hope that offers for employment would pour in for a man more than halfway to retirement. Remarkably, my husband had three interviews within the first few weeks, raising our hopes. Each one, however, ended in rejection. Determined to forge ahead regardless, my spouse asked the prospective employers for their reasons why he hadn't been hired. Their responses were game changers.

The first employer reluctantly disclosed that he had been put off by what seemed like arrogance during the interview, as if my husband were claiming to know how things ought best to be done. Lack of humility, the man explained, indicated someone that might not be a team player.

Right, we thought, so much for the "I am the answer to your company's prayers" approach. The second employer rejected my husband's salary request. We added "greed" to our dismaying list of unacknowledged character flaws. We felt as if we were living some twisted version of "Goldilocks and the Three Bears": first he was too hot, now too cold. The third employer admitted that the fit would have been "just right," except that my husband displayed a lack of enthusiasm for the job. His demeanour during the interview no doubt reflected his depressed and weary spirit. That evening was a low spot in our lives. My husband's identity, far from being affirmed, was depleted, "I am super-geek" replaced with "I am arrogant, greedy, and ungrateful."

Yet, it was in this severe shaking of my husband's roles-based identity that God finally got our attention. With little choice but to own these accusations, we went out for our evening walk and morosely began to confess our newly-highlighted sins. "*Lord, we confess that we are arrogant and—*" We got no further; it was as though God held his hand against our lips. Our confession was appropriate, but it wasn't what God wanted from us at this point. He wasn't interested in hearing who we perceived ourselves to be, either positive or negative. Both our initial defensiveness and our subsequent self-recriminations betrayed how much we allowed ourselves to be defined by roles of our own choosing. We measured our worth and our success based on how successful we were in our careers. Our roles, while not insignificant (in fact, unavoidable) had become the way we defined our identities. So much so, that we could not identify ourselves apart from them.

Instead, God began to speak to us of his divinely-appointed identity for us: who we were according to his perception, who he created us to be, who he was calling us to become. The sins of arrogance, greed, and ingratitude had been highlighted by way of contrast. He wanted us to re-define ourselves according to his blueprints; he created us to be a humble, generous, and grateful people. First Peter 2:9 captures that calling well: "*But you are a chosen people, a royal priesthood, a holy nation, God's special possession, that you may declare the praises of him who called you out of darkness into his wonderful light.*" This was, in essence, a call to "become" more and more who we actually are.

Roles alone should not define us. When he was banished from his home, Moses discarded the roles of both prince of Egypt and deliverer of Israel, and humbly served as a sheep-herder in the Midian wilderness. The debacle following his killing of the Egyptian soldier broke him out of a roles-based identity and left him a blank slate, waiting for God to write upon. The conflicting voices in his head from his adoptive and biological families vying for dominance over his life ceased to echo in the cavernous quiet of the desert. Perhaps God knew that Moses would need forty years of silence to escape their clamour.

We can all be deafened by the voices of family, friends, peers, church culture, and the media, jockeying for position and demanding to be heard. It is when we are most unsure of ourselves that we pay the most attention to those who, themselves, pay the most attention to us. Affirmed, we glow. Flattered, we preen. Loved, we surrender our identity to the one whose love we covet. It's likely that each of us can remember someone in high school who seemed to always have a boyfriend (or girlfriend) on their arm. With each new partner, they would change their hair style, clothing style, or even language. I watched one girl go from biker chick, to grunge, to preppie, to tragic artiste, all according to whomever she happened to be dating at the time. Entertaining for me; exhausting no doubt for her.

We all want to be liked, popular, and admired. But, even if we manage to set aside a roles-based identity, we may often find ourselves finding our identity in relationships, playing to whichever crowd we long to join and asking them, "Who do you want me to be?"

RELATIONSHIPS: WHO DO YOU WANT ME TO BE?

We had been meeting weekly for months now, yet Sarah had done little to break free of the patterns of abuse in her marriage that were scarring both her and her two young sons since they had returned from the mission field in south-east Asia. Her hands cupped the now-lukewarm latte as an expression of defeat suffused her features.

"He's a good dad," she seemed to be pleading with herself now. "He loves his family."

"He kicked a vacuum cleaner down the stairs and called you 'useless,' Sarah," I reminded her bluntly. "And scared the crap out of the kids."

"I know I should do a better job cleaning the house." My friend looked around helplessly at the dusty chaos of their home. "It was different before we had kids—I never had this much to do. I need to get on top of it all; he has a point."

"Is that the way you want your sons to 'make a point' with their future wives?" I asked. Sarah glanced up angrily, but I went on. "Is that what you really want for them, Sarah? For yourself? Is that who you have become?"

"What can I do?" she cried out. "What choice do I have? I love him, and divorce is wrong! It's all such a mess. We used to talk. Now he just comes home from work and watches TV. He's angry all the time. I don't even know who he is any more." She began to weep. "And I don't know who I am, either..."

"I'm not saying to divorce him. But Sarah—enabling him to be abusive is not loving him, it's actually harming him. He loves his family; why not use that leverage to encourage him to get counselling? Maybe he can figure out who he is, who God wants him to be. And you, too—you need to find what God has for you apart from being a wife and mother, find out who 'Sarah' really is."

The look she gave me was bleak. "Who I am? I have no idea." Sarah covered her face with her hands, weary and spent. "What if," she said hoarsely, "I'm not anyone?"

***

"I am because we are." This popular saying attributed to the African philosophy of Ubuntu illustrates the community-mindedness of majority world cultures. In contrast to the Western definition of identity defined by *roles*, we have here identity defined by *relationships*. Each member of a community is deemed valuable and significant, regardless of what (if any) contribution they make. Thus, the mechanic, the teacher, and the hunter stand together with the child, the disabled, and the aged. Occupation or role is secondary to the intrinsic value of person. Identity in this context is defined according to one's relationship within a community.

To a degree, this is true of any culture, as every individual has their identity affirmed by others' responses to our expression of Self: loved or rejected, honoured, or dismissed. We carry an identity based on the responses of those around us from childhood, when our identities were shaped by our parents. Later we refine this sense of Self through understanding our family roots, values, and structures. As our peer groups or communities accept us as individuals, we retain a healthy sense of self-worth. And if not? We will seek community wherever we can find it, settle for whatever intimacy we can get—including the intimacy of abuse. We prefer any interaction to the abyss of non-existence. We would rather, like my friend Sarah, be called "useless" than be called nothing at all.

THE FACEBOOK FACADE

In this age, many seek validation online. However, even with all the technology that allows us to be "connected" with others, there is also a new set of parameters that keep real relationship at a distance. Everything we post on social media is curated according to how we *want* to be identified, and the relationships that form based on those assumptions often fall short of being authentic. We are moving away from "I am what I do" in search of identity defined by "I am who we are," but we are doing this within the context of a technologically "contrived" community. Ultimately, this leaves us vulnerable to allowing others too much power in defining who we are.

Author and missiologist Reggie McNeal points out the urgent need to have our identity and calling clearly defined and in focus at all times, saying that "Not coming to a clear understanding of what you have been called to do leaves you vulnerable to completing agendas and imposing personalities in your ministry world."[12] We paradoxically want both intimacy and independence, an unfulfilled yearning behind the texts and tweets from those of us who desperately seek to be affirmed in our identity through the additions to our "friends" list.

---

[12] Reggie McNeal, *A Work of Heart: Understanding How God Shapes Spiritual Leaders* (San Francisco, CA: Jossey-Bass, 2011) 106.

And yet such definition can just as easily destroy our sense of Self, as we experience frequent cruelty, criticism, or indifference from peers, parents, and patrons alike. Inevitably, we fall short of the expectations of our virtual community, our actual community, and our own idealized self-image. We are always more than others perceive us to be, yet we often allow ourselves to be defined by others' perceptions. This can have disastrous results in anything other than a healthy, affirming community

It did for me.

THE COMFORT OF THE FAMILIAR

"Don't!"

Without intending to do so, I suddenly swatted my uncle's hand away. I had never objected to his public groping before, but somehow today, on my twelfth birthday, it suddenly seemed wrong. His heavyset face suffused with annoyance.

"What's your problem?" He snapped angrily. "All of a sudden you're a princess?" He shook his head, chewing on the ubiquitous, foul-smelling cigar. "Jeez. She used to be a sweet kid. When did she become such a brat?"

Disappointingly, both my parents and my maternal grandmother, present in the room, seemed likewise appalled at my outburst. It would be years before I realized that this family dynamic was far from normal, but in that moment I felt chastened, as if I had embarrassed them all. I was letting them down, being someone other than the good, submissive little girl they wanted me to be. The unfamiliarity of my actions bewildered them and frightened me.

What if they didn't like me anymore?

***

My earliest memories are lonely ones. I recall, even as a toddler in a crib, feeling a sense of abandonment. My mother married young, at nineteen, then waited nine years to have her first child (my brother) and five more to reluctantly birth me. It was twenty-eight years before she disclosed this reluctance to me, yet even as a child I sensed the absence of maternal bonding. Her second pregnancy was complicated by a large cyst that grew next to me in the womb. As it grew to the size of a grapefruit, not much smaller than my own head, there was fear that it might rupture and endanger both me and my mother. When my aunt told me this story, I finally had an explanation for my childhood nightmares of floating helplessly while being buffeted by massive balloons that threatened to suffocate me. My mother delivered both baby and "balloon" safely, but motherhood was not a role that my own mother relished.

When I was six weeks of age, my mother decided that they needed a "break" from parenthood and left me with her older brother and his wife for several weeks. Clearly, I have no memories of this time, but my alcoholic uncle became a prominent figure in my childhood, sexually abusing me into early adolescence. My father, whom I adored, also touched me inappropriately at times, but I had no grid with which to perceive this as anything but normal. I was a sexual object, smart enough to please the teachers, but unworthy of any particular investment of time or money or relationship. And so, from conception I was thus "defined" by these relational expectations, being whoever others wanted me to be, in hopes that I would be loved and accepted.

Unfortunately, such distorted identities broadcast like a neon sign over one's head on the playground; I was bullied by my classmates. My relationship with my mother was horrendous, and I left home at eighteen to relieve the stress on us both, while she threw dishes in hysterics. There followed a series of unhealthy relationships, rejection, anger, eating disorders, the usual array of social dysfunctions. This is the norm for those who have grown up accepting the labels that others choose for them.

STICKY LABELS

We are all affected by others' opinions about who we are; we are susceptible to praise and vulnerable to criticism. Labels can stick whether we want them to or not. Peeling them off requires an intentional effort, but it is important that we allow only the Namer to name his creatures. Any identity taken from others' praise or criticism is misleading at best, since such responses are based on the subjective reactions of the ones critiquing us and are not a reflection of who we actually *are*. Even affirmation, while it seems personal, is often only a reflection of how well we are meeting others' expectations at any given time. In their book, *Leadership on the Line: Staying Alive Through the Dangers of Leading*, authors Ronald Heietz and Marty Linsky allude to the tension that is created when we allow ourselves to take too much identity in meeting the expectations of others. They write:

> To anchor ourselves in the turbulent seas of the various roles we take in life, professionally and personally, we have found it profoundly important to distinguish between the self, which we can anchor, and our roles, which we cannot. The roles we play in our organization, community, and private lives depend mainly on the expectations of people around us. The self relies on our capacity to witness and learn throughout our lives, to refine the core values that orient our decisions—whether or not they conform to expectations.[13]

Affirmation ought not to define us; likewise, criticism need not derail us. Criticism is, at worst, rooted in envy and malice. At best, it's an encouraging reflection of how well we're engaging over an issue, suggesting that at the very least we are worth reacting to. But it's still painful when we allow ourselves to take a sense of self-worth and identity from others' opinions and then experience rejection. Painful, but hardly surprising. When we allow ourselves to be named according to accolades or criticisms, we anchor our identity in transient, fickle emotions. The very ones we are seeking to please may suddenly turn on us, as they did on Moses.

Moses, no doubt, learned the hard way that he couldn't depend on fickle emotions to define his sense of Self. Hoping to be lauded as a hero, he was instead hunted as a murderer. And yet, it was in this exile that he was prepared for the exodus to come.

---

[13] Ronald A. Heietz and Marty Linsky, *Leadership on the Line: Staying Alive Through the Dangers of Leading* (Boston, MA: Harvard Business Review Press, 2002) 187.

FROM EXILE TO EXODUS

Both affirmation and criticism are not without some value: they get us moving. As a community of believers, we are encouraged to build each other up, affirming those traits and behaviours deemed to be wholesome and righteous, so that we might *"...spur one another on toward love and good deeds"* (Hebrews 10:24). God may also use criticism to help us avoid taking our identity from any source other than him, for the isolation that often follows criticism can promote a candid self-evaluation and drive us back to the only reliable source of true identity. Time spent in exile can prepare us for change, for the exodus ahead.

Both Moses and Jesus experienced criticism and rejection, serving in both cases to create a divinely-designed separation and isolation from all who attempted to label them. How we respond to criticism is crucial in deciding the direction of our lives, whether we move towards bitterness, self-pity, and false identity, or towards deepened self-awareness, maturity, and God-given identity. It is not easy; the journey from exile to exodus is uphill.

My identity as a victim was not, I think, God's desire. It became familiar enough that I was terrified to stray outside of it. I suffered from claustrophobia and panic attacks in social settings, convinced that I did not belong in "normal" society, and could never fit in or be accepted. Therapists say that we comfort ourselves with the familiar, even if the familiar is destructive and dysfunctional; I was "familiar" with rejection and abuse.

Consequently, I found myself sabotaging friendships before I could be rejected, and thus had few friends. I found hope when I converted to Christianity in my late teens; perhaps now I could "belong." Unfortunately, I met few peers who hadn't grown up in healthy, happy, shiny Christian homes, and they could not understand my brokenness any more than I could understand their poise. I was anxious and tried to keep as busy as I could so that I would be surrounded by what passed as "normal" in mainstream church circles. Even in the midst of significant times of crisis, I refused to stop my volunteer work, fearful of falling off the fellowship radar. I was afraid, as with my friend Sarah, that if I did not have others around me constantly affirming my identity, I might cease to be.

Others, faced with similar circumstances, might react with defiance, determined to assert themselves and decide their own destiny. Such confidence eluded me until well into my twenties. At that point I fell victim to yet another lie, the popular conviction that that we can, alone and unaided, define ourselves and achieve fulfillment. This deception of self-actualization only prolonged my exile.

SELF-REALIZATION: I AM WHO I CHOOSE TO BE

Ryan shook his head. "It was just a dream, but it seriously messed with my head, you know? I had to pick one watch from this box of watches, and they were all totally different from each other. There was the heavy-duty sports model; you know the kind, like for scuba diving and shit. Astronauts even use them in zero gravity. Serious hardware." He grinned at the memory. "Then there was this solid gold Rolex, and some chunky pimped-out number with chains, totally awesome. At the bottom of the box I found one that was woven from leather and grass. It looked like it belonged on the wrist of some like Masai tribesman or something." Suddenly he sighed, as if remembering his childhood in Africa. "I think I wanted that one most. It reminded me of, well, home, you know? I still miss it."

Ryan and his parents left the mission field when he was ten, when his mother's serious health concerns led them to return permanently to Canada. The culture shock and subsequent teasing at public school left him an angry, rebellious teenager. He turned to drugs to find a sense of acceptance from his peers, and became seriously addicted to cocaine, having difficulty sleeping because of vivid dreams.

"What made this dream into a nightmare?" I asked, curious.

Ryan raked a hand through his greasy hair, agitated. "Yeah, well. It's just that I wanted them all, y'know? But I couldn't decide which one was really 'me.' It drove me crazy. Stupid, isn't it? I mean, I guess it's up to me to choose, huh? Decide who I wanna be?"

***

Psychologists in the 1970s held to the opinion that individuals fall into two camps: those who believe that the things that happen to them are due to outside forces (external locus of control), and those who see themselves as masters of their own fate (internal locus of control). It seems that Western culture—if the prolific publications of self-help books are any indication—promotes the idea that we determine our own lives solely by our personal choices (internal locus of control). Self-realization is perhaps the most optimistic concept put forth by modern psychology. It is also another moving target, aiming at reaching internal satisfaction through external achievement.

Not surprisingly, those with such convictions tend to struggle with perfectionism, anxiety, and self-recrimination when they fail to live up to their own expectations. Yet nonetheless, we continue to believe that, ultimately, we can control our lives and define ourselves, claiming, "I am whoever I choose to be." Dreams and goals are certainly essential to identity. Without them, we lack vision, and have little or no sense of identity. All our dreams, we tell ourselves, can be fulfilled if we just work hard enough. Self-realization is the core value behind the so-called American Dream.

However, as admirable as this popular Western first world adage may sound, ambitious individualism often disappoints in the end. Even those who enjoy a political climate that is favourable to the pursuit of individual happiness do not always attain their dreams. The reality is that not all dreams are in fact attainable. Freedom to choose does not guarantee success. Middle-aged Mexican migrant workers are free to dream of becoming astronauts, but that goal is out of their reach economically, academically, and physiologically. My friends' son, currently wiry and conveniently diminutive, dreams of becoming a jockey. He lives in abject terror of a growth spurt that will put that dream outside his reach. Each dream, each *raison d'être*, shapes our sense of Self. Each disappointment warps and cracks the mirror we hold up to our fragile egos. What happens when ambitious idealism hits the wall?

When we realize that our dreams can't be fulfilled, we can face a shattering sense of loss, leaving us without any idea of who we are or who we might become, only a frightening void and a bitter echo of what might have been. This crisis is often experienced by older men in the work force, who suddenly find themselves unemployed and no longer relevant or employable in their field of education and experience. Certainly, this was the case with my own spouse, as previously mentioned. His chosen career path was derailed by the fluctuations of an unstable global economy and the burden of his own, all-too-human inadequacy. The reality is that independent self-realization is often little more than an entertaining philosophical concept. In actuality, we are at the mercy of our own context.

CREATURES OF CONTEXT

There is an argument to be made that none of us is ever completely free to choose our identity. Whether one is a Calvinist, Arminian, or Semi-Pelagian in theology, most of us concede that, while we have some degree of free will, it's always affected by external influences and always warped by internal sinful tendencies. We cannot truly be independently-minded, objectively free of these influences. We may think we're making independent decisions in our quest for self-actualization, but, in reality, our decisions are often influenced by our environment. We are creatures of context.

Expressive Individualism, the modern conviction that we can—and must—be the authors of our own success stories, drives us to isolate ourselves from community, avoid seeking wise counsel, resent authority figures, and reject anything that isn't our own original idea. In this manner, we end up with less of an identity and more of an "I-*don't*-ity," basing our sense of Self on the rejection of any status quo. The ability to take initiative in the face of opposition is admirable—the classically American "can-do" spirit, for example. But in the extreme it can mean refusing to be led by anyone, including God. In this regard, the theology espoused by Western churches strongly reflects Western values of individualism. In his book, *GloboChrist: The Great Commission Takes a Postmodern Turn*, Carl Rasche writes, "The dominant culture of the West since the eighteenth century has been secular and individualistic, convinced that the supreme goal of human life and human history is the private pursuit of happiness and the guarantee of distinct individual political rights."[14] Anglo-European interpreters of the Bible over the last two centuries have limited the significance of the gospel to address the concerns of the individual, as opposed to corporate, societal, or communal application. Justification is expounded only as a transaction between God and an individual.

In contrast, the incarnational mission of Jesus involves becoming part of a people, a family, and a team. It involves being led by the Holy Spirit, submitted to a Lord, committed to community discernment, beliefs, and practices. Missional "sent-ness" is antithetical to independence. Lone Rangers make dangerous missionaries.

We actually depend on culture to give us a starting point to understanding ourselves, as it shapes who we are. Ideally, God uses culture to refine our hearts, equipping us to be in turn shapers of the culture in which we live. Unfortunately, we rarely factor God into the illusive equation of the self-made man or woman. If we don't acknowledge and co-operate with a God who desires to use our environment to shape us, we become helpless victims of circumstance. We nullify our ability to make unaffected, independent choices through our own ignorance of what the choices actually are; without an understanding of God's direction, we live in a grey and foggy reality, like a man who seeks to dress himself in the dark. Yet many are determined to do so, fumbling for the vestments that will adequately clothe them in their identity of choice, fully convinced that they'll somehow succeed.

THE MYTH OF THE HUMAN POTENTIAL MOVEMENT

We've been taught to believe that our highest calling is fulfilling our human potential. Even the Church holds to this, encouraging us to see how we can be empowered by the Spirit to "be the best *you* that you can be." While a resolve for self-improvement is laudable, in reality the freedom to choose our identity does not exist, despite rallying cries to the contrary. Left to our own resources, our claim to become whomever we choose is laughable. Even if we were to achieve our ultimate potential, we are like the church at Laodicea:

---

[14] Carl Rasche, *GloboChrist: The Great Commission Takes a Postmodern Turn* (Grand Rapids, MI: Baker Academic Press, 2008) 17.

You say, "I am rich; I have acquired wealth and do not need a thing." But you do not realize that you are wretched, pitiful, poor, blind and naked. I counsel you to buy from me gold refined in the fire, so you can become rich; and white clothes to wear, so you can cover your shameful nakedness; and salve to put on your eyes, so you can see. (Revelation 3:17–18)

The world (and popular Christian self-help tomes) urges us to discover our potential, develop our strengths, and thereby fulfill our destiny. In contrast, the Bible calls us to humbly acknowledge that, even at our best, we are indeed "wretched, pitiful, poor, blind, and naked."

Moses, fleeing to the desert, was helpless to self-actualize. He was alone, friendless, a wanted man. Arriving at a well in Midian, he only desired to stop running, to sit in the shade and grieve the fact that he had lost not one, but two homes. He watched silently as the daughters of the Midianite priest Jethro came to draw water. But, he did not speak to them. Indeed, men did not address women in that context. But, when the women were prevented from drawing water by the obnoxious shepherds that drove them away, Moses stood up.

It would, no doubt, seem ironic to him even then. Having failed to be a hero in either the Hebrew or the Egyptian culture, here he was trying to rescue these damsels in distress. It might have ended just as badly, but at this point he had nothing left to lose, and nothing to prove. It would hardly improve his image or allow him to return to Egypt to help these women, but it was clearly the right thing to do. The story goes on:

When the girls returned to Reuel their father, he asked them, "Why have you returned so early today?" They answered, "An Egyptian rescued us from the shepherds. He even drew water for us and watered the flock." "And where is he?" Reuel asked his daughters. "Why did you leave him? Invite him to have something to eat." Moses agreed to stay with the man, who gave his daughter Zipporah to Moses in marriage. (Exodus 2:18–21)

By giving up on trying to find identity in the good opinions of others, Moses inadvertently became the hero he always tried to be. It's a bitter-sweet moment; the opinions of these strangers and nomads held no weight for him. Their commendations, even the hand of the priest's daughter, would not heal his wounded heart.

GOD WHO CLOTHES

Our true identity is not a right that we can claim, or a potential that we can develop, but a garment that we are given. Ephesians 4:24 tells us that we are to "...*put on the new self, created to be like God in true righteousness and holiness.*" It is God who clothes us. Rather than attempting to uncover these qualities lying latent within ourselves, and seeking to develop them through self-actualization, we must receive what God gives us. Why else would Paul say that God had counselled him with the words, "*My grace is sufficient for you, for my power is made perfect in weakness*" (2 Corinthians 12:9)?

The only identity that Moses was able to self-actualize was that of an outcast, a stranger in a strange land, a title he both assumed and bequeathed to his first-born son. He had to wait another forty years before God finally called out to him by his name and clothed him with his true identity. Barefoot before the burning bush, Moses learned that his name had power to confer identity only when spoken from the lips of the Almighty. All he thought himself to be ceased to matter. Everything he thought he knew, his entire perception of reality, changed forever.

We who would seek to define ourselves, whether through roles, relationships, or self-realization, assume that we have a grasp on reality. Yet the fact is that none of us can see as God sees. Our perspective of reality, and thus our ability to perceive ourselves clearly, is tainted by our cultural environment, personal ambitions, fears and insecurities, and our sinful, fallen nature. We are not free to objectively self-actualize. We cannot "achieve" our identity; we can only receive it. We may identify our strengths, develop them, even design a destiny around them, but, as Moses learned, our strengths do not define us.

God alone has that right.

CHAPTER FOUR
Who Does God Say I Am?

"My name means 'Victorious warrior!'" the towheaded youngster piped up proudly. Next to him, a dark-haired girl smiled shyly.

"I was named after my great-grandmother. 'Claire' means 'clear, bright, and famous.'"

"My mom says I'm in the Bible," the next student boasted proudly to his class. "Michael is like an angel, and he's super strong, just like Batman!"

I watched my daughter falter when her turn came round. "I'm Robin," her voice was barely audible. "Like, like... you know, like the bird." Predictably, the classmates laughed and she recoiled. Mom to the rescue.

"And what a bird!" I exclaimed. "The boldest, bravest, most cheerful bird that ever was! Why, in the prairies it's the robin that comes first to encourage us that spring is on the way when the other birds are still too cold and wimpy to even think about singing!"

It took a few minutes to explain to these youngsters what a Canadian prairie winter was like, and why they should admire a bird with enough determination to drive its beak through an inch of permafrost looking for worms.

"Whoa..." they murmured, looking at my daughter with new respect. Robin sat back, relieved to be recognized for the spunky little creature that she knew herself to be. Identity crisis averted.

***

Later, snuggling up on the sofa, Robin asked me why we had given her that name. The answer, a true one, was that God named her, not us. When we prayed and asked him what the nature of the child would be, we saw courage, cheerfulness, spunk, and sweetness. Anyone who has watched the first robin arrive in a Winnipeg spring will understand our choice. So did Robin. God named her Robin because that is who she was in his sight.

What if we were to affirm that "I am who *God* declares me to be"? Spiritual formation is both a divine and a human activity. It's important that we be defined by a sense of personal calling, rather than only by function or task (as in: "I am what I do."). This sense of divine calling supersedes the self-realization of personal ambition (as in: "I am who I choose to be"), for, ultimately, personal identity through calling must come from *outside* of the sphere of human Self. "Calling" occurs when we allow our identity to be defined by the one who calls us, our Creator.

Our challenge lies not so much in resisting definition by culture, roles, relationships, aptitude or the myriad personal profile tests available, but in somehow aligning our perspective with that of our Creator, to see who we are in God's sight. Allowing God to be the primary defining force of our identity involves far more than being familiar with basic Christian values, biblical principles, and current Christian trends; it involves a dynamic disciplinary journey that may well both break and unmake us, so that we might be re-created to reflect the image of God, each of us in the unique way God intended. We will find ourselves forced to relinquish all faulty and futile attempts to define who we are until, as with the Israelites who stood before God unadorned and convicted with their golden calf, we stand before our Creator nameless, seeking to become the people that God has destined us to be.

Yet how can we receive this identity if we we focus instead on defining ourselves based on our roles, our relationships, and our striving towards self-realization? How can we hear our name being whispered when we are determined to shout it out ourselves? Again, only God knows us well enough to define us. Only the Creator can define his creatures. To receive this identity, we must first either relinquish, as Jesus did, or else have stripped from us, as was the case with Moses, all pre-conceived, faulty, and incomplete notions of Self, and allow God to tell us who we truly are. He alone is the *Namer*.

THE NAMER OF ABRAHAM

Choosing a name is rarely casual. All cultures have, at their core, an understanding that names carry significance, and perhaps even impart significance to their owners. Many biblical leaders had a moment in which their names were modified, or they were given new names altogether. In Genesis 12, we read of God's call to Abram to leave his country and venture forth to a new, promised land that God would show him. With this command comes a promise:

> *I will make you into a great nation, and I will bless you; I will make your name great, and you will be a blessing. I will bless those who bless you, and whoever curses you I will curse; and all peoples on earth will be blessed through you.* (Genesis 12:2–4)

This faith-filled man is seventy-five years old when God promises him that his descendants would be "...*like the dust of the earth, so that if anyone could count the dust, then your offspring could be counted*" (Genesis 13:16). But, as Abram grows older and remains childless, he wonders whether his servant Eliezer of Damascus will by necessity become the "heir" to fulfill this divine promise (Genesis 15:2–3). In Genesis 15:4, God tells Abram that he will have a son from his own flesh and blood.

However, Sarai doesn't have patience to wait for God to fulfill this promise, and so gives her slave, Hagar, to Abram (Genesis 16:2) to conceive and bear a son, Ishmael. Abram is eighty-six years old when Hagar gives birth to Ishmael (Genesis 16:16). There is no record in the Bible concerning the thirteen years of Abram's life following Ishmael's birth, but we can assume that, during this time, Abram is reconciling himself that this boy will be his only heir.

After these thirteen years pass, when Abraham reaches ninety-nine years of age, God again appears. Perhaps, understandably, Abram still doubts the promise, and so, in this encounter, the Lord takes the role of the great Namer, and redefines Abram forever. God changes Abram's name:

> *"I am God Almighty; walk before me faithfully and be blameless. Then I will make my covenant between me and you and will greatly increase your numbers." Abram fell facedown, and God said to him, "As for me, this is my covenant with you: You will be the father of many nations. No longer will you be called Abram; your name will be Abraham, for I have made you a father of many nations. I will make you very fruitful; I will make nations of you, and kings will come from you.* (Genesis 17:1–7)

One year later, Isaac is born. Abram's name, which means "exalted father," may have been a painful reminder of his inability to produce an heir. But now, he receives a new name that expands his identity beyond himself and his immediate circumstances to embrace a far-reaching vision that won't be fulfilled in his lifetime. He is now *Abraham*, "father of many nations." He is given an identity that has no foundation in his own strength or capabilities. On the contrary, it serves to remind him of his own inadequacies and weaknesses and rests in God alone. Abraham knows he is named well beyond who he actually is. Yet he has been named by God, and in humility and faith he becomes Abraham.

Likewise Sarai is given a new name:

> *"As for Sarai your wife, you are no longer to call her Sarai; her name will be Sarah. I will bless her and will surely give you a son by her. I will bless her so that she will be the mother of nations; kings of peoples will come from her."* (Genesis 17:15–16)

She is to be the mother from whom a multitude of kings and nations shall spring. God gives them both new names to force them to look well beyond themselves. This is how God names us, and scripture abounds with examples of others encountering the Namer of humanity.

JACOB: THE ONE WHO WAS ABLE

Jacob, the "supplanter," is renamed *Israel* when he finds himself in a desperate struggle with the Angel of God. Injured, clinging, and fearful of the confrontation yet to come with his estranged brother, Jacob comes to the end of his own strength. We read his story in Genesis 32:26–28 (NASB):

> *Then he said, "Let me go, for the dawn is breaking." But he said, "I will not let you go unless you bless me." So he said to him, "What is your name?" And he said, "Jacob." He said, "Your name shall no longer be Jacob, but Israel; for you have striven with God and with men and have prevailed."*

Jacob, the self-reliant, self-made man, is now disabled, helplessly dependent, and in need of a blessing he knows he can neither merit nor manipulate. He becomes, like Abram, named "beyond" himself; he is "one who wrestles with God and prevails." Here there's a paradox, for clearly Jacob hasn't bested the angel in this wrestling match. In fact he's been rendered helpless, weak, a loser in the battle. And yet God affirms that he has "prevailed." How can this be?

The word translated here as "prevail" is the Hebrew *yakol,* meaning "to be able." This word is not commonly used to describe vanquishing a foe or besting an opponent. Jacob did not *defeat* God. He wrestled with God, and "was able" to do so; he was *able* to wrestle. His only victory is that he met God's challenge, and in so doing found himself clinging to the One whose blessing he so desperately needed.

As with Abraham, Jacob is given a new name that both exalts, inspires, and humbles. Both Abraham and Jacob receive new names that make them poignantly aware of their own weakness. They are completely reliant upon the One who named them to make them worthy of the identity into which they are being called.

ROCKS, ENCOURAGERS, AND SONS OF THUNDER

Jesus's new name for Simon, *Peter*, is as paradoxical as the choice of "father of a multitude" for the childless old Abram. Simon bar-Jona became *Petros* (i.e., Peter); *Cephas,* in the Aramaic language (Matthew

16:18, Mark 3:16, Luke 6:14, John 1:42). As John 1:42 indicates, the words *Petros* and *Cephas* are synonymous; both mean "rock" or "a stone." Was Simon given this name to describe his rock-solid, steady nature? Was it a nickname?

Nicknames were no less common in biblical times than they are now. For example, the renaming of the sons of Zebedee as the "Sons of Thunder" likely reflected an accurate assessment of their personalities and dispositions (possibly as seen in Luke 9:54). In the same way, the surname Barnabas (Son of Encouragement), which the apostles gave to Joseph of Cyprus (Acts 4:36), was likely a reflection of his personality and spiritual gifting. However, Cephas/Petros was hardly illustrative of Peter's personality. On the contrary, we might well speculate that Peter may have been the Bible's first well-documented case of ADHD.

The man was impetuous, fervent, foolish, and fearful, hyperbolic in his promises, spectacular in his failures. He dared to lurch towards Jesus on the violent waves, and then nearly drowned when he realized his danger. He refused to let Jesus wash his feet, but then demanded that his whole body be washed when Jesus rebuked him. He had no impulse control. In Matthew 26:33–35 we read of his passionate but shallow resolve to follow Christ whatever the cost: "*Peter replied, 'Even if all fall away on account of you, I never will… Even if I have to die with you, I will never disown you.'*" Not long afterwards, he lies, not once but three times, denying his Master outright. We could even imagine that, faced with the lame beggar in Acts 3, Peter's "*Stand up and walk!*" may have elicited a brief moment of self-deprecating humour: "Oh no, not again. What did I just say…?"

Jesus's new name for Peter, "Rock," seems more indicative of his calling for Peter, rather than any attributes Peter himself possessed. Like Abraham and Jacob, Peter was named beyond who he was, in himself, capable of becoming. It is also significant that Peter's new name comes in the context of him answering a question regarding Jesus's own identity. Matthew 16:13–19 reads:

When Jesus came to the region of Caesarea Philippi, he asked his disciples, "Who do people say the Son of Man is?" They replied,

"Some say John the Baptist; others say Elijah; and still others, Jeremiah or one of the prophets." "But what about you?" he asked. "Who do you say I am?" Simon Peter answered, "You are the Messiah, the Son of the living God." Jesus replied, "Blessed are you, Simon son of Jonah, for this was not revealed to you by flesh and blood, but by my Father in heaven. And I tell you that you are Peter, and on this rock I will build my church, and the gates of Hades will not overcome it. I will give you the keys of the kingdom of heaven; whatever you bind on earth will be bound in heaven, and whatever you loose on earth will be loosed in heaven."

While the other disciples answered Christ's query literally, naming various figures thought to have been somehow reincarnated in the person of Jesus, Peter answered by describing the essence of who Jesus was: the Messiah, the Saving One, the Son of God. Jesus was more than could possibly be expressed by a simple moniker; he was beyond naming in the way that others were attempting to name him. Peter somehow knew this, and Christ's response is to declare Peter blessed. That's when Jesus changes Simon's name to Peter, perhaps emphasizing that this new name is also a "revealing" and a supernatural event. The implication seems to be that Peter's new name cannot be revealed or merited by "flesh and blood," but only by God alone. Peter's new name is not a reflection of who he *is*, but of who he is *called to be*. Peter is named beyond himself, beyond his own strength. In the naming, there is power, but it isn't the power of flesh and blood. It's the power of the Namer.

The Creator alone has the right to impart true identity to his creation. Roles, relationships, and self-realization all fall short. What we accomplish is transitory at best, as the opinions of others are subjective and unstable. Human will alone cannot fulfill human potential, for without God we are wretched, blind, and pitiable. We cannot achieve our identity, but we can receive it. Will we seek God for our identity? Then it's certain he will name us. But, even when we receive name, a calling, and destiny, we may not automatically become who God intends us to be. We may either *assert* or *abdicate* our calling.

THE ABDICATION OF ELI

The coach, Ron, and I laughed as we reminisced. "I remember when David first shot off the bench and launched himself straight into the defensive line," Ron chuckled. "His ankles were so weak that the skates were at a forty-five-degree angle to the ice."

I smiled at this memory of my son. "Well, in all fairness, he had never even skated before. All the other boys had been skating their whole life, it seemed. Typical Canadians, born to it; we're the imports," I reminded him. There were few ice rinks in Bolivia or Mexico.

"Yeah, ten years old and never been on the rink." Ron snorted suddenly. "Still, right from the start he thought he was God's gift to hockey."

I nodded, smiling quizzically. "You never burst that bubble, Ron. Not you, not the other coaches, not the parents, not even his teammates. You let him think he was hot stuff on skates when, frankly, he kind of sucked. Weren't you worried that he would let the team down, cost us the game?"

Ron laughed. "Well, I prayed a lot!" he said. "But I figured if we let him go on believing it long enough, he would become who he thought he was. And, you know, he actually did!"

***

Ron chose to agree to David's perception of himself until that perception became a reality. David, our youngest, did not self-actualize (although he did work mighty hard on his skating); rather, it was Ron's resolute heart and deliberate support that enabled our son to become an asset to his team. There is a Hebrew word, *kabed,* that describes the way Ron chose to strengthen his own positive perception of David's skill, and how David also chose to uphold that identity for himself. The word appears in 1 Samuel 2.

During the theocracy of Israel, various judges ruled. One, who was both judge and priest in Shiloh (where the ark rested for many years) was Eli. He had two sons, Hophni and Phinehas, and adopted the boy Samuel, who would later rise as a great prophet. Eli appeared to be devout and godly, but he was, without doubt, a poor father. His sons indulged in gluttony, eating food dedicated to God, and partook in sexual liaisons with temple prostitutes. They dishonoured their father, their people, and their God with their sinful behaviour.

Rather than deal with them as their sins deserved, Eli was passive, and merely rebuked them feebly, to no effect. Their sins, while not uncommon in the day, were more heinous in the context of their calling as priests of the Lord. Eli, Hophni, and Phinehas had received a divine calling, but they were not living according to who God had called them to be. Instead, they disdained and abdicated their God-given identity in exchange for an identity of base and profane self-gratification. We read of God's response in 1 Samuel 2:29–30:

> *"Why do you scorn my sacrifice and offering that I prescribed for my dwelling? Why do you honor your sons more than me by fattening yourselves on the choice parts of every offering made by my people Israel?" Therefore the Lord, the God of Israel, declares: "I promised that members of your family would minister before me forever." But now the Lord declares: "Far be it from me! Those who honor me I will honor, but those who despise me will be disdained."*

Later we read that, not only did God slay Eli's sons, he forever disassociated their family name from the priestly line. They abdicated their divinely-defined identity and lost it forever. What can we learn from this tragic story? We cannot afford to be casual about God-given identities. Once named by God, it is in our best interests to live according to who God says we are, and honour him by having faith in his perspective and plan for us. The identity we choose to receive will in fact determine how our lives unfold. God says, "*Those who honor me I will honor, but those who despise me will be disdained.*" The word "honour" used here is the Hebrew *kabed,* which can describe weight or heaviness, including the "weight" of significance or importance we give to something. We are to ascribe "weight" or importance to God and to his words, allowing him to define us. God calls us kings and priests in this world. If we live in this identity, we *become* who we really *are.*

Conversely, if we choose to "give weight" to our own selfish desires and sinful nature, God will "disdain" us. An ominous thought. Later, we will see how this brings about Pharaoh's fall when Moses demands that the Hebrews be set free.

The danger is there for all of us if we abdicate our responsibilities and take the path of least resistance, rather than accept the challenge to become who God calls us to be. Leaning into our God-given identity is hard work. Our son David was convinced that he was an athlete. We, along with David and his coach, had to "give weight" to that conviction until he finally became, if not Wayne Gretzky, then at least a more than decent offence. It didn't just happen; it's not always easy to mould ourselves according to Divine DNA. Human nature, sin, entropy—so much works against us.

DIVINE DNA

My spouse was disheartened after being convicted by God of arrogance, greed, and ingratitude during that last period of unemployment. Yet God assured us both constantly of our identity in his sight, and we knew that we had to somehow co-operate with him in claiming that identity. We worked hard to "give weight to" our God-given identities. It was rough going for a while.

In the light of 1 Peter 2:9's affirmation that we are a "royal priesthood," we tried to practice the dormant character traits within our divine DNA that we knew must be there. We gave thanks as we walked, our expressions awkward and stilted at first. We thanked him for daily bread, for home and hearth, for the loving handclasp we shared each day, for his big-ness in the face of our small-ness, for life and limb, and breath and eternal hope. Within the hour our spirits began to lift; we returned home with renewed hearts and found that we suddenly had energy and motivation to love on our children, to enjoy them, and to be generous in our attentions with each other.

Ideally, I would now write that my husband found a job immediately, that we have walked secure in our divinely-defined identities ever since, and that we are now living Happily Ever After. Alas, ingrained habits of false identity are not so easy to shrug off. In the months of unemployment that followed, our spirits often plummeted. But, we were determined to walk in this new version of self-hood; we did not want our own story to parallel Eli's. And so, the "thanksgiving" walks continued, often several times a day, according to our levels of anxiety. Sometimes we were hard-pressed to "feel" grateful, yet we doggedly gave thanks for everything God provided: birds, trees, friends, health, functional cars, the parting of the Red Sea (we were definitely scraping the bottom of the barrel that day). We gritted our teeth and tithed, hosting suppers for new immigrants from Latin American countries that like to eat lots and lots of beef. We sent our youngest to camp, planned elaborate birthday parties on a shoestring budget, and answered the phone no matter how much we wished to avoid the person calling, knowing that their needs would and should be allowed to interrupt our self-absorption.

God's people, we knew, were meant to be generous. We learned that living generously was about far more than money. It was about experiencing firsthand the truth in the refrain from "The Wonderful Cross": "O the wonderful cross, O the wonderful cross/ Bids me come and die and find that I / may truly live." Slowly, we began to internalize this outward change, choosing to live as though we really were the people God created us to be. And yes, we changed.

There were challenges, of course. No character change can truly be owned without first being challenged and fought for. Once my husband was employed, the financial stability lowered our guard, and over time we realized that it was more and more difficult to assert God's definition of our true selves. It was much easier to allow ourselves to be defined by our roles (employed, unemployed) or by others' opinions. Our identity in Christ, we realized, had a tendency to leak. We had to intentionally and continually overcome the temptation to find identity in our work, any work. But it was essential that we did so. We could either be overcomers, or else be overcome ourselves.

OVERCOMERS, OVERCOME

Any identity to which we choose to "give weight" will ultimately overcome us, but to be overcome by the Spirit of God is a powerful and life-giving experience. To be overcome by base definitions of Self degrades the *imago dei* and buries us alive. The result is a kind of spiritual paralysis that renders us incapable, in our own strength, of any real change. Our hearts become hardened, unable to believe or to move towards God's vision for us. If we choose instead to both believe and practice our God-given identity as kings and priests, a royal and chosen people, then we'll be free to become who he designed us to be. If we instead choose to give weight to other identities, they will dominate us and, in the end, cause us to lose any remnant of desire to be anything other. Like Eli's sons, we'll lose not just our lives, but our eternal inheritance.

The battle is real. We must overcome both selfish ambition and apathy. Some of us will be eager to co-operate, thrashing as we already are in the panic of an identity crisis. Others of us are secure in our complacency, settled in the roles and relationships we've chosen to define us. For these, leaning into a God-given identity is painful, systematically stripping away all that we cling to, all that gives us confidence and courage. We may experience wrenching loss as we exchange the familiar for something new and alarmingly strange.

God desires to name us beyond who we are, beyond who we can become in our own strength. How does this happen? How can we co-operate with the Almighty in this renaming? Like Jacob, we must confront the one who overcomes us, becoming overcomers as we wrestle to surrender to his will and cling to him for blessing. We must humble ourselves and acknowledge that we are wretched, blind, poor, and totally dependent upon the one who names us instead of stubbornly pursuing self-realization. The process may be painful, frightening and, for a time, we may find ourselves adrift, abandoned, and alone.

Just like Moses.

CHAPTER FIVE: MOSES
Who Was He?

Jen's voice was calm, but contained an undercurrent of deep fear. She'd been leaking amniotic fluid for hours, and the doctors at the hospital hadn't been able to detect a fetal heartbeat. They advised her to either stay and have an induced abortion, or simply go home and allow "nature to take its course."

Her voice caught as she related this to me over the phone, then became urgent and low. "I know it seems hopeless, but I am convinced that this child is meant to live. Eddie has already given up; he says the baby is dead and he refuses to pray or allow himself any false hope. It's like he has already buried this baby! What happened to his faith?" Back from the mission field, Eddie and Jen were struggling in their marriage, as the solid conviction of their previous calling and identity faded in the harsh light of financial and health issues, adding to their profound sense of loss. And now their baby was at risk.

"We're here for you, Jen. What do you want us to do?" I asked.

"Pray! Pray with me right now; bless this baby with life, with healing. My husband may have given up, but I never will. This kid needs someone to believe in him!"

***

Jen gave birth to her second son seven months later. The doctors were dumbfounded. Somehow, the amniotic sac sealed over, and the fetus continued a normal gestation. Micah was a healthy, normal baby boy. With one notable exception: he never bonded with his father. Try as he might, Eddie was never able to cultivate a relationship with his son. Although he clearly loved his child, it seemed that, having once deadened his emotions to the fetus he believed lost, he couldn't cross that chasm and bond with the child that now lived. Micah was a high-strung child, and, over time, manifested a moderately severe anxiety disorder and learning disability. His mother blamed this on the stress he had suffered while in the womb, and the emotional withdrawal of his father during the pregnancy. The marriage did not survive.

Micah went on to become a fine young man, but, like Moses, he had a rough start in life. Both suffered even while in the womb. After all, in terms of *in utero* distress, there could hardly be a greater tension that carrying a baby to term, knowing it was destined to be sacrificed violently to foreign gods.

AN OFFERING FOR HAPI

In Egypt during the fourteenth century BCE, Jochebed would not have had a more stressful pregnancy. Married to Levi's grandson, Amram, she had already borne him two children. Their first child was a girl by the name of Miriam; the second child was Aaron, now aged three to five years. Their childhood was far from normal. Three hundred or so years had passed since Joseph first brought the Hebrews to the land of Goshen, and the Egyptians were concerned that the Israelites were growing too numerous, becoming a potential political threat. And so the Egyptians elected to put the Israelites under hard, servile labour in order to subdue and control them.

By playing on the fear and distrust of outsiders, the Pharaoh of the day, as with the likes of Hitler and other dictators, exploited an opportunity to create a powerful sense of national unity, grounded in animosity towards a common foe. Pharaoh portrayed the Israelites as a national threat of epic proportions, capable of endangering Egypt's security and way of life if, in the event of war, the Israelites should ally themselves with Egypt's enemies. Pharaoh then addressed this fictitious threat with a threefold strategy.

In Exodus 1:11–14, Pharaoh enslaves the Israelites by taking away their privileged status. Then, to restrain their growth as a nation, Pharaoh instructs midwives to kill Hebrew boys at birth. The midwives ignore his instructions and tell him that Hebrew women give birth before they can even arrive, so Pharaoh commands that all Hebrew baby boys be thrown into the Nile River (Exodus 1:15–2:10).

Pharaoh encouraging the Egyptian people to throw Hebrew babies into the waters of the Nile was a stroke of political genius. Egyptians worshipped the god Hapi, the guardian of the Nile, not in temples, but at the river itself. They made offerings to Hapi by throwing food, amulets, animal sacrifices, and valued objects into the river to petition for the yearly flood that would make farming these desert lands possible. Pharaoh could convince the Egyptian people that they were actually ensuring the fertility of their land, securing the future survival of their own children, averting famine, and appeasing their gods. It was a reasonable atrocity. Genocide usually is.

But, for the Hebrew slaves, it was a nightmare. Jochebed and Amram's fear could not help but be transferred to their children, including the one in the womb. Could they hear the cries of infants and toddlers in nearby streets, being killed by coldly efficient soldiers? What went through Jochebed's mind when her own contractions began? Was she desperately hoping for another daughter to be born, a child that would have a hope and a future?

But, Moses was a boy. The moment of his birth would hardly have been greeted with shouts of joy; he was doomed. Did Jochebed and Amram dare to bond with their babe, knowing that his life would inevitably be cut short? Did they "disengage" emotionally during the pregnancy, as Micah's father did, sure that their child would not survive? Perhaps. But at some point, following his delivery, they were faced with the unthinkable. And, rather than despair, they decided to fight for his life.

Hebrews 11:23 tells us that, *"By faith Moses' parents hid him for three months after he was born, because they saw he was no ordinary child, and they were not afraid of the king's edict."* That they *"were not afraid"* is, perhaps, less of a reflection of their emotional state and more a statement on their resolve to defy Pharaoh's edict and keep their baby alive. It could not have been easy.

The three months in which Jochebed kept her infant son hidden would have been tremendously difficult and tense; it's unlikely that they allowed the baby to cry or make much noise. Miriam and Aaron would have been warned to keep their baby brother a secret; it's possible that their mother kept them sequestered indoors, as they were young and unreliable. The very act of having to "hide" this reality would have been a stressful burden for these children to bear. It's unclear how the genocide was carried out, but we can imagine periodic raids by the Egyptian soldiers, breaking into homes, ripping innocent babies out of the arms of their distraught mothers. Was there screaming in the camp? Were the wails of infants suddenly, horribly, silenced? Were the Hebrews there when their children were thrown into the Nile? The images are beyond bearing.

Every day would have been torture, with Jochebed wondering when her son would be discovered, when his tiny, perfect form would be torn from her breast and sacrificed to the god of the great Nile. Imagining these things, as no mother could help but do, Jochebed came up with a radical, outrageous idea.

Jochebed chose not to wait for day when her son might become a cold corpse floating in the Nile, but instead took action and placed the baby in the river herself. It was a terrific risk, and the ironic symbolism of this act is staggering. Jochebed could not keep him, had not, perhaps, even yet named him. But for this boy to become the man that God intended, to receive his divine identity and calling, she had to let him go completely. She had to, in effect, abandon him, set him adrift, and trust in God's plan. Yet, if Jochebed had not chosen to surrender her control over her son to God, Moses might never have fulfilled the destiny God had for him.

Not all mothers would have this kind of courage. I certainly did not, and it almost cost me the life of my own first-born.

THE GOD OF THE NILE

Earlier, I briefly described some of the dysfunctional aspects of my childhood. Not surprisingly, I had very few healthy role models, and my only definition for "normal" was within the confines of my own birth family and the parameters of a frightening Western urbanity.

By the time my first son, John, was born, I had added a legalistic perspective to my emotional baggage. I was convinced that the only hope I had of raising a child in the ways of the Lord was to shelter, even isolate, him from the potentially harmful influences of a dark and evil world. I dreamt of raising my children in the rural villages of South America. Instead, we ended up in a low-income urban housing complex in Surrey, B.C., strewn with garbage and hypodermic needles. Ironically, it was when we managed to move to a more affluent neighbourhood that John began to show signs of wanting to wrestle himself out of my anxious clutches.

At the first sign of misbehaviour, I panicked. I had to save him from the world, save him from the god of the Nile that wanted to destroy and devour him. Like Jochebed, I tried to "hide" my son. This strategy was not born of faith but of fear, and it went on far longer than the three months of infancy during which Moses was hidden.

John was seldom out of my sight and virtually never outside of my control. We did not own a television for many years, and, when we had one, we carefully avoided most shows, diligently muted all commercials, and allowed only children's videos of our own choosing. My thinking was, "If it's popular, it's probably bad." Play dates were virtually non-existent; I trusted no one. We attended a small, charismatic church that, although alive within its own walls, was relatively isolationist; we worshipped using only songs composed by those within the denomination and had little or no interaction with the global Church community outside of that. We were, indeed, an island unto ourselves.

When John reached school age, we pinched pennies to send him and his sister to a private Christian school, but because of the general level of affluence of its attendees, most of his classmates were far too busy with after-school music, dance, gymnastics, lessons, tutoring, family ski trips, and cruises to allow for much social interaction outside of class. And so, within the social context of our low-income housing complex, our children felt awkward in their ignorance of popular TV show jargon, video games, and common playground obscenities. Added to that, within the culture of the private school, they had no grid for the vernacular of mainstream "Christianese," did not know the songs played on popular Christian radio stations, and felt intensely embarrassed that they wore second-hand uniforms, couldn't afford extra-curricular activities, had never learned to ski, and spent vacations domestically with their mom and dad at local parks.

Our parenting style devolved into a long list of "don'ts" that severely curtailed our children's growth and social development. We did little to bolster their sense of Self or build confidence in them, neglecting the team sports or similar activities that might have helped them recognize and develop their strengths and as-yet-unrecognized talents. In short, as parents we instilled in our children what amounted to a strong sense of "I-don't-ity," rather than identity. Without realizing it, we inadvertently set them up to experience the kind of rejection and ridicule that could traumatize them at least as effectively as the emotional and sexual abuse of my own childhood.

It was, as my mother-in-law would say, a "disaster waiting to happen." And when it did happen with our oldest son, it happened, quite literally, with a bang.

LET ME GO!

By the time John was sixteen, his behaviour was openly defiant. Facing one of our many periods of financial crisis, we had withdrawn our children from the private school and, with much trepidation, enrolled John in a local high school. This did not help matters. His misbehaviour escalated, as he became more and more drawn into a party lifestyle, acting out with lies, fits of anger, and the kind of activities that leave a mother quaking with anxiety.

I vacillated between guilt, rage, and terror. Was this all my fault? Nurturing guilt, I would easily get trapped inside my own self-pity, making the situation all about me and my feelings of failure. At other times I would begin shaking with fury, feeling that I was being manipulated and blackmailed by my own child. "Let me go or else," he seemed to be saying. "See what I'm capable of doing?" I deeply resented this and reacted by denying him more and more of the very freedom he craved. At the same time, I was howlingly afraid for his future, both immediate and eternal. In dishonouring both us, as his parents, and our values, was he rejecting God forever? At what point might God stop pursuing him? Thoughts like these would pull me into a dark and twisted place, where life itself seemed pointless. If I could not save my son, what use was I to anyone?

As John continued to rebel, his lies became rote and our relationship crumbled. We scrambled for leverage, using threats, tears, and bribes to keep him under our thumb. We would offer something he wanted in hopes of winning back his heart. Then, in the wake of a surge of his defiance, we would withdraw whatever we previously agreed to. It was a roller coaster ride for the whole family, without—as my youngest says—any of that "woohoo!" factor.

On one memorable occasion, when we snatched back a promised freedom that we felt he no longer deserved, John punched a good-sized dent in the wall and stormed off. I recall feeling a sense of foreboding, but convinced myself that we were just being Responsible Christian Parents. I also recall thinking, "Well, I guess there is no doubt now about who he is."

John was "bad."

That night was a milestone, in the worst of ways, as his misbehaviour reached a painful climax. Later, broken and ashamed and utterly defeated, I knew I had reached a crossroads. I had no strength to continue trying to control the Cosmos. Grieved nearly beyond sanity, I knew I had only two choices: give up or give over. By God's grace and my husband's stern love, I chose the latter, although it would be a painful and circuitous path for the next three years as I fought to keep my hands from once more clutching and choking my son's free will.

It was time to put my baby into a basket and launch him into the Nile. I had tried to hide him long enough. Babies and young children need us to control their environment, to keep them safe. But control is a terrible thing if it goes on too long. Sixteen years was far too long for me to hide my son from the world. Being controlled in this way had left John feeling like he had no freedom, no value, no choices, and that I was taking over in defining his identity. I knew I needed to stop.

But neither could I simply give up and wash my hands of him. Instead, I needed to give him over—over to the tumultuous and dangerous river he had chosen, and then watch and pray like stink. Would God be there and meet him in this river? There were no guarantees. He might sink. He might be rescued. Or he might just swim away of his own accord. There was little faith in my weak, croaking prayers that day. Just enough to utter them.

Jochebed was a far better mother than I. Although she hid her babe for three months, she knew that, sooner or later, he would be found and taken away from her by force. Every mother faces that fear; I was no different. I was afraid that the world would take my son away from me, that sex, drugs, crime, violence, and sin would rip him out of my arms and destroy him. I wish that I'd known that there was only one way to keep my child safe. I needed to do what Jochebed had done.

Remember that Jochebed did not wait for the soldiers to come and throw her child into the Nile River. She knew it would happen, one way or another. So, instead of waiting fearfully, she decided that she herself would be the one who would place him, carefully and intentionally, in that very same river. It was a terrible risk—it *is* a terrible risk—to deliberately expose your child to that which can corrupt and consume him eternally. But parents cannot really keep their children safe forever, nor are they meant to. Children cannot grow in a bubble, and they cannot learn to know, trust, and follow their Creator if we, as parents, refuse to trust them to God. Further, although God surely does not want us to be part of the evil in the world, neither does he want us to withdraw and be separate from the world. In John 17:15–18, Jesus prays to his father that we would not share in the evil *of* the world, but is very clear that he is sending us to be *in* the world. A royal priesthood, a nation of leaders that would change that world. We read:

> *My prayer is not that you take them out of the world but that you protect them from the evil one. They are not of the world, even as I am not of it. Sanctify them by the truth; your word is truth. As you sent me into the world, I have sent them into the world.*

How do we do this with our children? How can we send them into the world, knowing that they will not allow themselves to be defined by the world? What did Jochebed do?

BABY IN A BASKET

Jochebed did not throw her baby into the water. She wove a basket of straw to keep her child afloat, and then carefully, lovingly, launched her son with her own hands. Then, crouching behind the reeds and sending her daughter Miriam to follow the fragile craft, she watched. Still, alert, anxious, trusting, watching to see what God would do. She was ready to respond to the slightest event.

We so often hear that we need to "wait" on God. For Jochebed, as for us, waiting was not meant to be passive inaction, but a state of heightened awareness and readiness that likely cramped her muscles and burned her unblinking eyes. She had done all she could to keep Moses alive, afloat, safe. Now she watched to see what would be required of her next.

As parents, we weave a "basket" for our children with our prayers, a delicate but unsinkable lifeboat to keep our children from sinking as we launch them into the world. The Nile River is a powerful metaphor for a dangerous, wild, and treacherous world, frighteningly out of our control. After we let our children go, we watch, crouched and alert, to see what will be required of us next. We don't let go, so much as we give them over. If the basket springs a leak or runs aground, our initiative is not to take back control, but to seal the tear and nudge them further into the waters. And we do this not once but continuously, until rescue arrives.

Jochebed did not abandon her baby, as my mother did me. Instead, she hid herself in the bushes and watched. We don't know how long she watched, afraid that he would drift, afraid that he would sink. Perhaps she was tempted to rush in and rescue him herself, but knew that such an act would only endanger him even more. She must have been desperate for someone to save him, terrified for his life. In the same way I feared that my son, once set free, might irretrievably drift away from the values of our family, drift into sin, and sink forever. Relinquishing control was shatteringly difficult.

COACHES AND CHEERLEADERS

This was a mistake, I thought, glancing furtively at the seedy office. The man in front of me must have been in his seventies. What was he even doing here, still presuming to be a guidance counsellor for inner city schools? What was I thinking, looking at enrolling my son in distance education? In the end I voiced my misgivings. This would be like homeschooling, I complained. Something I had sworn I would never attempt, even on the mission field. Better uneducated than murdered at the hands of his own mother.

"You listen to me now," the white-haired, wild-eyed academic prophet intoned. He shook his finger in my face, "You are not the coach here, you are the cheerleader. Your son needs you. Whoever he thinks he is, you cheer him on. Let me, life, and God in heaven adjust his course as need be. You just help him find out what he's good at. Your job is to help John find out who he really is, then let 'im go. Got it?"

Incredibly, I did, at last, begin to get it.

***

As I began online schooling with John, I was stunned to realize that he had both abilities and disabilities that I had never recognized. His reading comprehension was impeded by a moderate dyslexia and visual processing disorder inherited from his father. How had we all missed that? In other areas, he excelled. His struggle with the concrete sequential challenges of math were far outweighed by his phenomenal gifts of self-expression. His blatant lack of wisdom in, for example, choosing good friends, was offset by a sensitivity and insight into those same friends that astounded me with its depth. He knew them intimately; more, he understood them and had compassion for them. What did that mean, and what did it tell me about who John really was?

Long after he stopped using unhealthy means to cope with his anxieties and pain, John continued to bring a wide scope friends to our home, hoping to help them and heal them. This son that I had dominated into near non-existence was in fact a gifted and remarkable young man. I began to see who God had called him to be, apart from the identity that I had sought to impose upon him.

I did indeed need to learn how to "let 'im go." The question I often had was, hand him over to whom? Who would God send to rescue the baby in the basket? Would I be relieved or apprehensive about the rescuers that God sent? Jochebed had to face this concern as well, and it did not go as she might have hoped.

UNEXPECTED GUIDES

As our children grow, we parents step back and allow God to send other people into their lives to help guide them into adulthood. However, as this anxious Israelite mother found, it may not always be the person we would choose. God sent an Egyptian princess to rescue a Hebrew baby. Hardly what Jochebed might have seen as God's preferred future for her son! Imagine living during the Holocaust and having your children rescued at the last minute from the gas chambers and certain death, only to be adopted by a member of the Nazi party. Death might seem better than knowing that your child would be raised to believe heresy, learn to despise the values of his own people, reject the one true God, and be lost eternally. Watching her baby being lifted up into the arms of a daughter of her oppressor, Jochebed would have recoiled. It meant that her son might be raised in Pharaoh's court, taught to feel superior to his Jewish brothers, perhaps even to despise his own biological family. Whatever name or identity Jochebed might have had for her child was now in the hands of her enemy. Who would he become? How would he live? What would define his identity?

Sometime after the worst of our parental crisis, John found himself in an agonizingly long stretch of ambiguity in which he was neither fish nor fowl, neither saved nor reprobate, and he attended to his studies half-heartedly. By then, our charismatic church had died a lingering and sad death, and we optimistically moved our brood to a large church with the kinds of programs and resources we hoped would help impart health and sanity to us all. John held himself aloof from what he viewed as the privileged and shallow hypocrites of institutional religion. The youth pastor initially showed interest in befriending John, but it quickly became evident that they had no common ground whatsoever, and John was, by his own choice, left to brood in the back pew.

Then, an anomaly entered the conservative homogeneity of our mainstream evangelical congregation. With shaved head, pierced ears, and a comfortable middle-aged paunch, this man breezed into the office of our youth pastor's office one day to introduce himself. As the head of the theatre department at the local high school, and an effusive and radical Christian, he had daily access to numerous students and a reputation for taking the fringe element and leading them into an intimate relationship with Jesus Christ. He was convincing and sincere and would go on to baptize numerous teenagers in our church. Unfortunately, at that moment his reputation had not preceded him.

He brashly asked the youth pastor to give him a contact list of those young men in the church community who were "falling through the cracks." The pastor was taken aback and asked why he assumed there were such young men in the church. The reply was a gently derisive snort: point taken, but bad form. To his credit, the youth pastor overcame his initial suspicion and was humble enough to acknowledge that yes, there were a number of young men with whom he was having some difficulty establishing an effective rapport. This visionary literally held out his hands and said, "Give them to me, I want them."

John's name was high on the list. When we met the teacher in question, we were as put off as our youth pastor had been. His approach came across as brash, liberal, and contemptuous of authority. He was perfect for John. But like Jochebed, we were alarmed that God would use this person, who seemed to flaunt so many of our values, to be the one to help our son. But by then, God had been speaking to us of the need to surrender control, so we gritted our teeth and told the man, "Go get 'im." And so, the basket was drawn out of the waters of the Nile.

Within months, John began attending a loosely-structured Bible study where relational authenticity was the highest value. He thrived in this environment of raw honesty and mentorship. Later, he would admit that it probably saved his life. John also brought several of his friends along, and his mentor perceived leadership qualities in them all. Within a relatively short time, John had so grown in confidence (and, yes, brashness, liberal-mindedness, and contempt for authority, but hey...) that he volunteered to become a youth leader in our church.

We fought our tendency to criticize and correct, remembering the advice: we were to be cheerleaders, not coaches. Sure enough, there were plenty of hard knocks to come, with more than enough coaches to confront John and help him to grow. In the five years that followed, John had several other influential men come into his life: employers, mentors, peers. Some were hardly a mother's first choice, not being entirely free of what I called "the cringe factor," yet together they were able to take John through his next phase of growth in ways that we, as parents, could not.

Like Jochebed, we crouched nearby, watchful and prayerful, ready to do whatever we could to co-operate with God's plan for our son. We watched constantly for any opportunities to speak into John's life. Those opportunities often came at the most inconvenient hours of the night, but we always welcomed the chance to affirm his identity. Our vigilance and alertness was at times exhausting but, in the end, imminently worthwhile. To our amazement, we even found ourselves in a position to mentor many of those who were mentoring John, which did much to assuage our fears about their influence over him. God gave us indirect ways to care for our son and help to shape the forces that were themselves shaping him.

Jochebed's waiting and watching was also rewarded. As she crouched in the reeds, the opportunity for action presented itself to Jochebed in a wonderful way. The Egyptian princess who drew him from the waters recognized him as a Hebrew and called for a wet nurse. Bingo. Miriam, who had been watching, leapt to her feet. She knew just the woman! And so Jochebed was hired to nurse her own baby, likely for up to four years, as was the custom in both Hebrew and Egyptian culture at that time. That meant up to four years of being able to shape and affirm his Hebrew roots.

The princess christened her adopted son "Moses," likely a derivative of *mose*, the Egyptian word for "son," and possibly in honour of her father, whom some historians postulate was the Pharaoh Thutmose II (more on this theory later). Alternate theories are that he was named *Mosheh* by his biological mother, either then or later, this being a Hebrew variation of the Egyptian word *mose*, which in turn resembled the word *Mashah*, Hebrew for "drew out," hence the reference in Exodus 2:10. It is also possible that Jochebed and Amram either gave him some other name at birth, or did not name him at all since they had little assurance of his survival. Regardless, Moses was in many ways a "nameless" baby boy until he was rescued from that river. It was only then that the long process of forming his identity began. But on route to becoming the leader that God intended him to be, this fragmented and conflicted soul struggled with confusion, wondering where he really belonged, and to whom. Before he found himself as God's child, he had to untangle his own complicated roots.

CHAPTER SIX
Whose Am I?

Judy looked down at her newly adopted infant son, who had been sleeping since they first placed him in her arms, happily oblivious to the fact that his entire destiny had just been altered. Her husband John had just run out in search of diapers, bottles, soothers, and other mysterious paraphernalia for the parentally-challenged. They honestly had no idea what they were doing. Judy felt sorry for the little fellow.

Then his eyelids fluttered, and he looked at her for the first time. This is it, she thought. Bonding time. She felt a sudden and unanticipated surge of deep affection.

"Hello there," Judy said quietly. "I'm your new mom." Then she rolled her eyes at her own lack of imagination. Cheesy. Ah, well, too late to come up with a better first line.

As if on cue, a look came over the baby's face that Judy later described as "rather confused." For all the world, he seemed to be saying "Who the heck are you?" Then, with furrows of perplexity creasing his perfect infant brow, his gaze seemed to turn inwards.

"So, if you're Mom," he seemed to be asking himself, "Then who was that other lady?"

***

Judy and John went on to adopt two more children in the years to follow and watched as each of them faced their own crisis of identity, amplified by the amorphous gaps in the biological time-line of their past. As parents, they did all they could to define and affirm their children through each stage of childhood and adolescence, both fascinated and frustrated by the interplay of nature versus nurture in the shaping of their behaviour and characters. As adopted children, they were, and were not, a reflection of their new family's ancestry.

Their quest for identity led them into, and out of, various relationships, academic pursuits, healthy and not-so-healthy lifestyle choices, depression, anxiety, medication, and therapy. Their parents' faith in God sheltered them in their journey through seasons of seeking, blaming, ignoring, missing, and then seeking again the God who created them.

In many ways, all the children have continued to be as quietly quizzical as the oldest had been in infancy, struggling with an ongoing search for a sense of Self. Judy and John look back on years of joy, stress, hilarity, grief, confusion—and they regret nothing. But it was complicated, they admit. Adoption often is.

MOSES, BUNDY, AND THE SON OF SAM

Statistics tell us that adopted children often have high rates of depressive and anxiety disorders. David Kirschner, Ph.D., is a psychologist and psychoanalyst with a private practice in Woodbury, Long Island, New York. As the founder and director of the Nassau Center for Psychotherapy, he is nationally and internationally recognized for his clinical and forensic work on adoption issues, often in high profile forensic cases of homicide. His book *Adoption: Uncharted Waters: A Psychologist's Case Studies* looks at abandonment, rejection, bonding, split-identity, and other adoption issues in what he has coined as "Adopted Child Syndrome." Although "Adopted Child Syndrome" is not yet included in the Diagnostic and Statistical Manual of Mental Disorders, it's generally recognized as a term for the common patterns of maladaptive behaviour in adopted children who exhibit serious behavioural symptoms. These children may be angry, argumentative, and often refuse to accept any personal responsibility for their aggressive actions or outbursts of rage. They may also be intensely preoccupied with their origins and the circumstances of their adoption, as well as hypersensitive to perceived rejection. Kirschner writes:

> We have found that, to one degree or another, virtually all adoptees experience a sense of loss and identity confusion... [They strive] to forge a clear and healthy sense of self, an integrated identity that is consistent with reality, while at the same time fortifying an image of themselves that they wish to project. For adoptees, this can be a more difficult and complex proposition, because of the gaps in their history and disparate, sometimes contradictory parental and self-images.[15]

In the vast majority of cases, adoptive parents are comfortable with disclosing the details of the child's adoption. Often, the children grow up to meet and know their biological parents, finding resolution and balance. However, in some dysfunctional situations, the adoption causes excessive stress to either the adoptive parents or the biological parents, or both. They may compete, acting out their own insecurities and seeking to manipulate or "buy" the child with material goods, attention, and indulgence. Contrarily, they may withdraw, or refuse to discuss birth history or the adoptive process at all, escalating the child's own anxiety and uncertainty. Both situations are damaging to the fragile psyche, as tension between the two sets of parents can precipitate a severe identity crisis in the child. This is especially true when the two sets of parents have strongly conflicting values, religious beliefs, and related opposing views on child-rearing, ethics, and morality. Knowing this, is it any wonder that Moses had a speech impediment?

Moses, remember, was rescued by a member of the enemy camp, as it were. His adoptive mother's people oppressed his biological parent's people and slaughtered their babies. In cases this extreme, adopted children might not develop a clear sense of right and wrong because of the conflicting paradigms around them, and subsequent moral ambiguity

---

[15] David Kirschner, *Adoption: Uncharted Waters: A Psychologist's Case Studies* (Woodbury, NY: Juneau Press, 2006) 8.

leads to even further inner turmoil. In addition to a conflicted sense of Self, these children may also have a deep sense of rejection—either imagined or real—as adoptive parents inadvertently or intentionally emphasize that they were abandoned by their birth parents. This sense of rejection can have profound consequences.

"Son of Sam" serial killer David Berkowitz claimed to have been deeply hurt when he felt that his biological mom had rejected him. According to biographies, killer Ted Bundy suffered a similar emotional trauma when he learned, at the age of thirteen, that he was an illegitimate child. These are extreme cases, obviously. The point, however, is that regardless of how attentive and caring both sets of parents may be, adoption is not an ideal state for developing a healthy sense of Self. The stress incurred may cause children to be hostile to either or both sets of parents, potentially leading to explosions of violent proportions. In the case of Moses, it's entirely possible that such inner tension precipitated the homicide.

Even if we were to presume that the Egyptian princess and the biological parents were loving, caring individuals and allowed Moses to have healthy relationships with both families, some degree of dysfunction was inevitable. In the case of his Egyptian family, there may have already been significant dysfunction, verging on being downright weird. To begin with, they were a rather inbred bunch.

A DISTURBINGLY CLOSE-KNIT FAMILY

Theories on the dating of the Exodus abound. Here is one more, albeit unlikely—that of the date for the Exodus falling in the 1400s BCE. Proposing an early date for this event is popular among biblical literalists, as we will see (I am not one). In actuality, an early dating for Exodus is probably beset by too many problems to be acceptable (Canaan until the 1200s was still under Egyptian control, leaving Joshua and the early part of Judges full of too many inconsistent historical references). Many more biblical scholars seem to favour a later date for Exodus, with Rameses the Great as the reigning Pharaoh of the time. Nevertheless, there are weighty arguments to be made on both sides, and some degree of conjecture is inevitable and, to be honest, fun.

To do justice to proponents of the early Exodus theory, let's unpack a little of the rationale. The Bible states that Moses led the Israelites out of Egypt four hundred and eighty years before the fourth year of Solomon's reign (1 Kings 6:1). The interpretation of the "four hundred and eighty years" as a precise period of time is uncertain, but biblical literalists insist that it is the sum of twelve generations of forty years each, as biblical generations tend to be recorded. Most Bible commentators do agree[16] that Solomon's reign likely fell during the tenth century BCE. Counting backwards from Moses's death at the age of 120 (although this too may have been a rounded number to describe three periods of forty years, as in three generations), including his forty years as a shepherd in Midian and his forty years leading the Israelites in the desert (Acts 7:23), it's likely that Moses was born in the late sixteenth to early fifteenth century BCE. For the sake of a glimpse into the kind of dysfunction that results from royal inbreeding (Pharaohs and offspring frequently marrying one another to keep the bloodline pure and the inheritance intact), let's embrace the speculative hypothesis of an early date for Exodus for now.[17] Regardless of which royal family actually did adopt Moses, it was likely to be at least as complicated and close knit as the one we are about to describe!

If we assume this early timeline, the ruling Pharaoh at the time of Moses's birth might have been Thutmose I, a military general who married into the royal line by wedding Ahmose, sister to the deceased Pharaoh Amenhotep. Amenhotep had died without an heir, but Thutmose I and Ahmose produced two sons and two daughters, all of whom died in childhood except for one daughter, Hatshepsut. Thutmose also fathered a son by a minor wife, Mutnofret; this son was married off to his half-sister Hatshepsut and then ruled as the Pharaoh Thutmose II. Such marriages between siblings or half-siblings was common for

---

[16] Gleason L. Archer, *A Survey of Old Testament Introduction* (Chicago, IL: Moody Press, 1974) 223.

[17] All dating proposed here is an approximation based upon archaeological evidence, bearing in mind that "...the Egyptians possessed no fixed system of reckoning time. The events which they desired to record chronologically were associated with certain regnal years of the pharaohs," George Steindorff and Keith C. Seele, *When Egypt Ruled the East* (Chicago, IL: University of Chicago Press, 1957) 6.

Egyptian royalty of the period. Historians write that this couple was unable to produce any children for some considerable time, possibly due to the weak and frail health of Thutmose II, or perhaps the inescapable difficulties in conception and pregnancy that occur in an incestuous relationship. They eventually had one daughter, Nefrure, but no son to be heir to the throne.

Given this timeline, imagine if the Egyptian princess who rescued baby Moses was actually Hatshepsut, daughter—and childless wife—of a pharaoh. If the rescuing princess was indeed Hatshepsut, then naming the baby "Mose" would have been akin to naming him "son." She may have even hoped to groom him as their heir, optimistically anticipating one day calling him "son of Thut" or "Thutmose" the III. In other words, it's possible that Moses was adopted into the royal family with the intent of raising him to take the mantle of the next pharaoh. Hatshepsut was certainly ambitious enough. As a maternal antithesis to Jochebed, this powerful woman both fascinates and repels.

Whether or not she was Moses's adoptive mother, Hatshepsut was, by all accounts, an extraordinary woman.[18] Her empty sarcophagus, found by renowned archaeologist Howard Carter in 1903, provoked a tenacious search for her body. Her mummy was discovered in 2007, and the ensuing forensic analysis included everything from CT scanners to DNA gradient thermocyclers to identify her lineage. She was found without a coffin, retinue of servant figurines, jewellery, clothing, or any of the paraphernalia associated with royalty. It was as though she'd been shamefully hidden, and this may well have been the case. Hatshepsut was, in fact, something of an enigma.

Sometime after her death, her images and cartouche (name symbol) were apparently chiselled off the shrine walls, her obelisks covered over with stone, and her name erased from public memorials. It would seem that this had been done by her surviving stepson, in an effort to eradicate the iconography of this monarch altogether. Hatshepsut herself inscribed her anxiety about public opinion and the preservation of her memory on an obelisk at Karnak, writing: "Now my heart turns this way

---

[18] C. Brown, "Hatshepsut; The King Herself," *National Geographic,* April, 2009, accessed July 2015, http://ngm.nationalgeographic.com/2009/04/hatshepsut/brown-text/1.

and that, as I think what the people will say... and speak of what I have done."[19] What was the source of this fear, the reason for her infamy?

HATSHEPSUT'S BEARD

Hatshepsut's husband Thutmose II died around 1504 BCE, likely from heart disease, according to subsequent CT scans of his corpse. Holding to our early Exodus date hypothesis, Moses would then have been approximately twenty years of age himself, certainly old enough to ascend to the throne if this was in fact Hatshepsut's intention and if he himself desired to do so. However, Hatshepsut's now deceased husband had, following in the footsteps of his father, sired a son by yet another "minor" wife. This child was Thutmose III, gender-destined to be the heir apparent. Hatshepsut had no intention of allowing this son of a rival wife to rule over Egypt, and she named herself Pharaoh upon her husband's death, ruling until her own death in 1482.

She was not the first woman to have done so. Others include Nitokerty (ca 2175 BCE) and Sobeknefru (ca 1760 BCE), previous queens who reigned as co-regent with sons or stepsons too young to rule alone. There is, however, no evidence that Hatshepsut's stepson was ever allowed co-regency. Hatshepsut did not want to share her power with anyone, it would seem. As the unchallenged queen regent, she excelled and ushered in a time of great peace and prosperity through renewed trade with surrounding nations. Her political skills may well have been admired. But Hatshepsut went well beyond the boundaries of political correctness in the twenty-one years that followed.

Reliefs show Hatshepsut performing decidedly male, kingly functions: making offerings to the gods, ordering up obelisks from the quarries at Aswan, and having statues chiselled that showed her in female form, yet with the striped *nemes* headdress, the *shendyt* kilt, and *uraeus* cobra that were the classic regalia of male kingship. She had herself named the "female Horus, Ruler of Upper and Lower Egypt, Daughter of Re," and used for herself the king's name "Kamare."[20] In her mortuary

---

[19] Joyce A. Tyldesley, *Hatchepsut: The Female Pharaoh* (London, EN: Penguin Books, 1998) 210.

[20] George Steindorff and Keith C. Steele, *When Egypt Ruled the East* (Chicago, IL: University of Chicago Press, 1957) 40.

temple, she is depicted as having been fashioned by the great god Amun, as his beloved daughter. At some point, in this assumed role, Hatshepsut began to wear a false beard, either to intentionally deceive others of her gender identity, or to accentuate her own authority. Hattie was a force to be reckoned with, indeed.

If this woman was in fact the princess who raised Moses, then she would have worn a beard when Moses was between the ages of twenty and forty years. Again, do the math. This means that, when Moses murdered the Egyptian soldier and fled to Midian, his Egyptian "mom" had already, in effect, become his "dad." If the resulting confusion weren't enough to permanently damage his psyche, it's at the very least conceivable that his implied speech impediment of Exodus 4:10 might have been the result of childhood and adolescent trauma (the Hebrew words are *k'vad peh,* "heavy of mouth," and *k'vad lashon,* "heavy of tongue"). With a childhood like that, Moses would have been lucky to walk away so relatively unscathed.

If this timeline were accurate, that would place Moses in Midian when Hatshepsut died. Her sickly stepson, Thutmose III, finally took the reins and proceeded to surprise everyone, eventually becoming one of the greatest of the rulers of ancient Egypt. He became a formidable warrior, referred to as "the Napoleon of ancient Egypt,"[21] leading at least seventeen successful military campaigns, one of which, the Battle at Megiddo, is still cited in military academies to this day. Once free from his stepmother's restraints, Thutmose III became a skilled soldier who brought the Egyptian empire to the zenith of its power by conquering all of Syria, crossing the Euphrates to defeat the Mitannians and penetrating south along the Nile to Napata in the Sudan. But for all that, he was likely a bitter, vengeful man. Meeting his adopted brother Moses again would, as they say, push all of his buttons.

If indeed Thutmose III was the Pharaoh of the Exodus, he would have found it intolerable to be bested by the aged, exiled Hebrew who had once been a privileged prince in his royal court.[22] The animosity

---

[21] "Ancient Egypt's Greatest Warrior: Tuthmosis the 3rd—Egypt's Napoleon," Royal Doc, https://www.youtube.com/watch?v=kO3VtjBjNm0

[22] Hershel Shanks, "The Exodus and the Crossing of the Red Sea According to Hans Goedicke," *Biblical Archaeology Review* 7 (1981): 42–50.

would be understandable. Angry at having been denied the throne, eclipsed by his bizarre stepmother, and likely jealous over her success, Thutmose III would have celebrated, not grieved, Hatshepsut's demise. And so, if she had ever shown any favour to Moses during his lifetime, that too would have been cause for intense sibling rivalry, for Thutmose III had been denied any such significance all his young life. His reunion with Moses would be fated to go very badly. There is some intriguing evidence to suggest just how badly.

Thutmose III reigned until his death in the mid-1400s BCE, which coincides with our proposed Exodus date. His first-born son, Amenemhat, predeceased his father. It's pure speculation, but not completely implausible, that this first-born son died in the last of the divine plagues of the in Exodus story. Imagine the rage that Thutmose III would have felt if an exiled Hebrew ex-con appeared to challenge him with some fictitious story of a God who speaks from burning bushes. Then, humiliated time and again, we can imagine Pharaoh's furious resolve to resist, to punish, and to maintain control at all costs over Moses and the Hebrew slave populace. Haunted by his past, Thutmose III was fighting phantoms, desperate to prove himself powerful. The death of his first-born son would have crushed him.

A second son, born to another wife of Thutmose III, later reigned as co-regent with his father. After the death of Thutmose III, this son became the Pharaoh Amenhotep II.[23] Whether his father's death took place when the divided waters of the Red Sea flooded his lungs, we do not know. But most certainly, he did not die a happy man.

Imagine the bitterness that existed between Thutmose III—a frustrated and impotent ruler for much of his life—and an adopted Hebrew slave that had once known such obscene favour, only to fling it all aside, choosing instead "...*to be mistreated along with the people of God rather than to enjoy the fleeting pleasures of sin*" (Hebrews 11:25). Whoever it was that adopted Moses, whatever the era, that person would likely never have understood how Moses could leave the splendour (and the weirdness) of Egyptian royalty behind. They would hold a fierce

---

[23] Aidan Dodson and Dyan Hilton, *The Complete Royal Families of Ancient Egypt: A Genealogical Sourcebook of the Pharaohs* (London, U.K.: Thames and Hudson, 2004) 132.

grudge. They wouldn't have forgotten that Moses murdered an Egyptian soldier. They would have gnashed their teeth at the pauper who became prince, only to throw it all away. And Moses was apparently more than willing—even glad—to do so. Why? Why would anyone embrace exile?

EMBRACING EXILE

Juan Carlos took his time describing the attendees of his Latin American immigrant support group. He wanted the pastor to understand their plight.

"These are educated men," he explained. "They came here for their children to have better opportunities in life than are possible in their native countries. One, he has his Master's in Electrical Engineering. He is working at the mushroom farms here in B.C. Another, he is architect; I think he is worried that his construction job is damaging his hands. There are two medical doctors also. One works at a bakery in assembly line, the other is stocking clerk in the hardware store."

"This is terrible!" exclaimed the pastor. "They must be so unhappy!"

"I think maybe they are lonely, yes. Because no one knows who they really are, no one sees what they do." Juan Carlos shook his head. "It hurts them when their own children do not respect them. Sometime the kids, they are embarrassed. They do not see that their parents, they give up everything to come here. But I don't think the parents are unhappy, no. Because they know what is el proposito—their purpose in the life."

"What would you say is that purpose, Carlos?" I asked.

"It is to die, every day, a little death for their children. Es un abrazo—an embrace." It was an embrace of their exile.

***

By murdering the Egyptian soldier, Moses became a marked man. Ironically, the Hebrews he sought to champion rejected him, even exposing his crime and putting Moses in more danger. This rejection would have cut deeply, for Moses intentionally gave up everything—

rank, power, security, a future—for the people who now rejected him. Just as our friend Juan Carlos related, the sacrifices we make will not always be seen, much less appreciated. Moses died "a little death" that day, running away from his own people. He had nowhere else to turn.

Moses fled. The Egyptians were after him, led by Pharaoh himself. Or, as we have speculated, Pharaoh "herself"! What was Hatshepsut feeling? Seeing her son reject her and all she offered, after everything she had done for him, might provoke any mother to madness. He must be caught and killed.

What was Moses feeling, besides fear? Was his pride wounded? He had rejected his royal future to side with his oppressed Hebrew kinsmen, only to find that his sacrifice was meaningless; his own people do not want him. Hatshepsut was nearing the end of her life and would in fact die only a few years later. Would Moses have turned back if he had known that the Hebrews would be oppressed another forty years under the vengeful hand of Hatshepsut's son? Bleak as their future might be, Moses only knew the bleakness of his own. Spurned by the one culture, and persecuted by the other, Moses is now not just homeless, but virtually nameless. No one claims him, no one thanks him, no one wants him.

The new immigrants that meet with Juan Carlos monthly speak of the isolation, the lack of community, and the sense of rejection that weighs them down daily as they labour at menial jobs in Canada. Yet they, at least, had the hope that their sacrifice would one day be appreciated by their own children. Moses had no such hope.

In Midian, Moses encountered yet another challenge to his identity. Though he was received favourably by the Midianites, he spent the next forty years immersed in a third culture, learning yet another language, assuming yet another persona as he became a humble shepherd.

His sense of isolation is keenly evident in the way he named his first child: *"Moses named him Gershom, saying, 'I have become a foreigner in a foreign land'"* (Exodus 2:22). This name comes from the root *garas*, meaning "to drive away," or "to banish." To be in exile. Moses named his first son according to his own sense of utter desolation. Alone, isolated, misunderstood as no human being ever was until Christ himself, Moses entered into a wilderness experience that stripped him of any remaining sense of Self. It left his soul raw, vulnerable, and ready to encounter a holy God.

Moses had no idea that, in embracing exile, he would become a typology of the Saviour that was to come after him, two thousand years later. Instead, he must have shaken his head, gazing at the desert land of his new home, and wondered what on Earth he was doing there.

CHAPTER SEVEN
What Am I Doing Here?

Like Moses, Jesus chose to embrace exile. He chose to abandon his royal abode in favour of a birth on Earth as a human babe. Jesus laid aside his glory without hesitation for the sake of those whom he loved. Like the Egyptian prince wiping sweat off his brow as he herded dirty, smelly sheep across an arid plain, Jesus left the glory of heaven itself to be swathed in scratchy, barnyard rags. Where Moses was set adrift in a straw basket, our Saviour chose a feeding trough (Luke 2:7). Did he, like Moses, ever look around in bemusement, wondering "What on Earth am I doing here?"

In Philippians 2, we read that Jesus humbled himself in spite of his divinity:

> *...in very nature God, did not consider equality with God something to be used to his own advantage; rather, he made himself nothing by taking the very nature of a servant, being made in human likeness. And being found in appearance as a man, he humbled himself...* (Philippians 2:6–8)

Though the cross was his final death, Jesus, too, died "a little death" every day to be among us.

Like Moses, Jesus was conceived at a time of oppressive rule; in his case, that of the Romans over the people of Israel. During the first century, Rome had dominion over Israel, after invading and conquering Jerusalem in 63 BCE. In order to keep control, Julius Caesar installed Herod as king. Herod had the favour of the new emperor because, as king, he expanded the Jewish Temple in Jerusalem according to a more Hellenistic-Roman design, imposed a sacrifice for the priests to give on behalf of Rome and the emperor, and renamed cities in honour of Caesar. But because he was obviously currying the favour of their conqueror, Herod was deeply resented by many of the Jewish people, who themselves paid dearly for the advancement of Herod's career.

Herod's building campaigns were made possible by heavily taxing the peoples of Galilee, Samaria, and Judea, to the extent that the majority lived in poverty. Not only were they required to pay taxes to the Empire, but they continued to function as a "temple-state" and pay the tithes and sacrifices of the Jewish religion. Decades of this economic oppression saw Jewish families falling increasingly into debt and facing the potential loss of their family inheritance of land. Despite the freedom to practice their religion, the Hebrews were essentially economic and political slaves to Rome. This was nothing new. Historically, they had been conquered by Babylon, Assyria, Persia, the Greeks, and now Rome. In their subjugated state, the Hebrews clung to their prophecies that God would send a prophet like Moses to lead them in a new "exodus" and set them free from oppressive rule. Enter Jesus.

The parallels between Moses, Israel's first deliverer, and Jesus, the final and ultimate deliverer of all humanity, are myriad. Jesus, like Moses, lived in a time of poverty, hunger, debt, and oppression. Moses was the initial founder of the divinely-designed culture of Israel, and Jesus was the Saviour who later ushered in the eternal Kingdom culture that Israel was designed to reflect—and both men shared personal histories of their identity being first surrendered, then imparted.

Both Jesus and Moses shared an identity of being "adopted"; Moses, reared by Egyptian royalty, and Jesus by his earthly stepfather and mother. Both maintained connections to their natural parents—Moses implicitly as he chose to identify with fellow Hebrew slaves, and Jesus explicitly as we see in his response later to the frantic scolding of his earthly parents after they later found him in the temple: "'*Why were you searching for me?' he asked. 'Didn't you know I had to be in my Father's house?'*" (Luke 2:49). Jesus, like Moses, received identities from both his earthly parents and his community. None of the labels "stuck" on Moses; he was neither fully an Egyptian prince, not fully a Hebrew slave or a Midianite shepherd. Likewise, no earthly identity could contain the Son of God—all fell short and left him "nameless."

Both Moses and Jesus had their identities threatened right from the moment of their birth. But, their respective identity crises were, in fact, a vital part of God's plan. It was crucial for their future ministries that neither allowed themselves to be defined by roles, earthly relationships, or personal ambitions.

DESTINED FOR GREATNESS

Jesus's identity was foretold well in advance of his birth. When the angel Gabriel comes and visits Mary to tell her that she will give birth to Jesus, he says:

You will conceive and give birth to a son, and you are to call him Jesus. He will be great and will be called the Son of the Most High. The Lord God will give him the throne of his father David, and he will reign over Jacob's descendants forever; his kingdom will never end... So the holy one to be born will be called the Son of God. (Luke 1:31–35)

The title "son of God" was, at that time, the very title Augustus claimed for himself. Caesar Augustus was called the "son of god," the "saviour" of the whole Earth who brought "peace" to Rome. The announcement of this was heralded as "good news" (Greek: *euangelion*). This was the political and religious propaganda of the day, much as in Egypt at the time of Moses, where the pharaohs also claimed to be gods. And, just as Moses proved the deity and sovereignty of the Egyptian rulers to be false, so Jesus made a mockery of the Emperor's claims to divinity in the light of the true *euangelion,* the arrival of the true Son of God, Saviour of the world. This was far more than a casual exercise in semantics; Caesar would have seen the challenge as a very real political threat. Or, as N.T. Wright puts it:

> From the start, Jesus' proclamation of God's kingdom was fighting talk... When Herod heard, he was angry; he was King of the Jews, and rival claimants tended not to live long. When the Chief Priests heard, they knew that it meant a challenge to their power base, the Temple. If Caesar had heard, he would have reacted similarly.[24]

At every turn, Jesus exposed the false identity of the rulers of the day by walking in his own God-given identity. Moses, as we will see, did likewise when he later returned to Egypt to confront Pharaoh. Both Moses and Jesus were destined for greatness through sacrificing their own identities; both had mothers who knew that their sons were far from commonplace. Both were conceived in difficult times, and both were born in less-than-ideal conditions, to say the least. For Moses, the birth experience was full of ominous threats to his life. For Jesus, his birth was equally lacking in any of the comfort and security that a mother could hope for at such a moment.

At the time of Mary's pregnancy, a census had been called—yet another taxation of an already over-burdened populace. Joseph, Mary's husband, was required to leave Nazareth and return to his hometown of Bethlehem to be registered. In Mary's late state of pregnancy, this would have been an arduous journey of eighty miles, taking up to one week to complete. By the time they arrived in Bethlehem, exhausted and anxious, the town was bustling and accommodations for travellers were hard to find. Scripture reports that there was no room for them in the *kataluma,* a Greek word meaning "guest chamber, lodging place or inn."

The biblical account tells us that Mary gave birth to Jesus in a shelter for farm animals and placed him in a manger, or animal feeding trough. This does not necessarily imply that Jesus was born in a barn; in the second century CE, Justin Martyr, an early Christian apologist, held that Jesus was born in a cave outside the town, and early church

---

[24] N. T. Wright, "God and Caesar, Then and Now," Festschrift for Dr. Wesley Carr, 2003.

tradition also favoured this view.[25] Either way it would seem, then, that Mary and her husband Joseph were housed, if not in a cave, then inside a domestic stable. It was likely relatively clean, but, nevertheless, not the first choice for a woman in labour, and Mary was probably keenly aware of the social prioritization given her. The delivery went well, and Jesus was born safely, but Mary's heart likely grieved at the venue.

This was a far cry from what Mary might have expected, having received an angelic visitation that she was about to birth a king. Did she doubt? Did she wonder whether this little boy really was the Son of God? Had it all been a hallucination, had Joseph's dreams confirming the identity of the child been just that—only dreams? Even when the shepherds, responding to angelic voices, came to the house and offered reassuring words of affirmation regarding the identity of this child, her relief would have been short-lived. Like Jochebed, Mary had little time for the luxury of celebrating the birth of her child.

OUT OF EGYPT

At the time of Christ's birth, there were, aside from the angelic heralds, other signs and portents in the heavens. Those wise enough to discern the meaning of the stars understood that a king had been born. Leaving their homeland, these Magi travelled to Jerusalem and there informed King Herod that they were seeking the newborn king of Israel. In a paranoid fit of protectionism, Herod commanded that all male Jewish babies be put to death, lest one of them pose a threat to his empire by growing up to usurp his throne (Matthew 2:16). Where Jochebed anxiously hid Moses for three months from a likewise paranoid Pharaoh, Mary and Joseph were warned in a dream to flee to Egypt, to hide in the very land where Moses was born (Matthew 2:13–15).

The parallels between Moses and Jesus are, as already mentioned, numerous. But none is so profound, perhaps, as that of identity. In their self-imposed exiles, both Moses and Jesus received their identity from God alone, allowing hardship and persecutions to shape them according to his purpose. For Moses, this meant forty years in the wilderness

[25] Joan E. Taylor, *Christians and the Holy Places: The Myth of Jewish-Christian Origins* (Oxford, UK: Clarendon Press, 1993) 99–102.

of Midian as a shepherd. For Jesus, it was an exile within an exile: a parallel forty days in the desert, being tempted by Satan, within the thirty-three years of his exile on planet Earth. During their exiles, both Moses and Jesus were offered attainable identities. Moses might have become an Egyptian prince, or at least a high-ranking general. He could have chosen to remain a reasonably well-off shepherd, son-in-law to Midianite priest. Instead he chose to identify himself as a stranger in a strange land until God called to him by name from out of the burning bush. Jesus refused to be provoked by Satan into proving his identity as the Son of God, choosing instead to wait and trust that God would, in time, define him both publicly and powerfully. He refused to stage a military coup, refused to become anything other than a servant to his disciples, refused to rip himself off the cross and destroy those who mocked him. Instead, they both waited.

Waiting for God to define us is a choice we can all make, co-operating with the divine Potter as he moulds us through trials, temptations, and rejection. Is it easy? Heck, no.

GET OUT OF MY SANDBOX

Hopeful but anxious, I raced out with the other grade one girls as the bell rang, uncertain of what we were supposed to do at recess. There was a brief instant where we all looked at each other with undisguised curiosity. Then the Alpha Female in the pack quickly established her authority (we'll call her "Kimmy").

Kimmy gathered the girls around her, bossing them with an easy confidence and utterly enviable poise. She clearly expected to dominate and, therefore, dominate she did. Her first coup was to declare a running contest, which she promptly won. Poised, perky, and athletic to boot. Go figure. I felt no jealousy at this point (that would come later, and in spades), only anxiety that I wasn't keeping up with the other girls.

Kimmy next announced that we would skip; we skipped around the schoolyard until I was exhausted. Then there was something called "wiggle dancing," which I did not understand and felt embarrassed by without really understanding why.

Collapsing on the corner of the nearby sandbox, I wiped sweat from my brow, panting. Kimmy suddenly glared at me, incensed. "Get out!" she snapped at me. "That's not your sandbox!"

Perhaps she interpreted my lack of proficiency in these activities as a lack of enthusiasm, or my inability to read social cues as a failure to know her rules. I will never know. Either way, something prompted her to propose the next game, "Run away from Nikki." Confused, I watched the other girls scatter, shrieking with laughter. When they stopped to regroup in the field, I assumed that this strange game was over, and jogged towards them, thinking that it would now be some other girl's turn to be playfully shunned.

To my chagrin, the girls bolted again the moment I reached them. Kimmy was on a roll. This happened three more times until, thankfully, the bell rang and I hurried back into the school, feeling a deep sense of shame.

The playground was not safe, the sandbox not to be shared with the likes of me.

***

Rejection is a particularly sharp-edged tool that, in God's hand, can carve out depths of character like nothing else. It almost seems, at times, that God sets us up for it. Moses was buffeted by conflicting identities from birth; Jesus was heralded by signs, wonders, and prophetic claims that guaranteed he was destined to be shunned, stoned, or worse. They could not fail to experience rejection at every turn. The playground would never be safe for them.

I've been told that evidence of early childhood trauma is a certain discernible social "aura," as it were. Others, particularly those prone to bullying—themselves wounded and angry and wanting to project that anger on someone weaker—are often drawn to those who have been emotionally damaged. As with the animal kingdom, predators seek to pick off the weakest member of the pack, the lone straggler that can't keep up. Certainly, this seemed to be the case in my own life. As early as grade one, I experienced a distinct and intentional rejection from my peers. Introverted, awkward, quiet, and (fatal flaw) academically bright, I found myself bewildered by that first recess. There were other incidents more hostile and aggressive, and at least two occasions where I was physically attacked and punched. The sense of defeat was cemented into my psyche from that day on, and I spent subsequent play periods hiding around the side of the school in self-imposed exile. But the painful rejection of my childhood and youth did not yield only bitter fruit, for it was in exile that I began to think that there was more to life than what I saw around me. There just *had* to be.

By the time I was in my teens, I had cultivated a taste for solitude and silence. There was little of either in my home; the TV blared incessantly and my first discovery of the lock on the bathroom door gave my mother hysterics. (What did she think I was doing in there?) I escaped during the warm months to a riverside park down our street and crouched in the long grass by the bank. I would there sit for hours, daydreaming, sketching, reading, and later, writing. When winter came and I was forced indoors, I sequestered myself in my room and did the same. Occasionally, I encountered a kindred spirit of sorts at school, and we would "hang out," but these were temporary interruptions in my reclusive life.

Left to my own thoughts, I contemplated spirituality. I explored the occult in its varied forms. I found there was indeed a realm of supernatural patterns and power that both drew and repulsed me. It was nameless and impersonal, and for this reason I instinctively viewed it as dangerous. Yet it was also appealing, promising me some modicum of control over the cosmos which had hitherto victimized me.

And so, I began to cultivate what I called a "neutral" spirituality, although I now know there is no neutral ground. Wicca fascinated me. I considered hallucinogens, but in the end shunned both alcohol and drugs. In retrospect, I attribute this to the early childhood trauma of seeing my father and uncle inebriated and unreachable. I recall pleading with my dad to "come back" when he was drunk, terrified of the emotional disconnect that seemed to create in him a kind of maudlin and sentimentalized insanity. He was not an angry drunk, but he was not "there," and that frightened me. I wanted no part of addictive substances; the thought of losing control terrified me. In fact, pretty much everything terrified me.

By then, my brother, who, because of our common social dysfunction, was my only friend for many years, had discovered his musical gifts, and although I enjoyed hearing him practice the classical piano pieces in the basement below my bedroom, I wasn't always welcome to interrupt. Irritating younger sisters seldom are! At times, my loneliness was intolerable. There were nights when I would stand barefoot in the snow outside our house with a wounded, desperate, inarticulate yearning. For what did I yearn? I had no idea. I railed at the silence, demanding a response from God, gods, animistic spirits, ghosts, and demons of the dark alike, and profoundly resented the lack of response from any and all quarters. Until, of course, the response came, as it inevitably must.

God wants to be found. His call on our lives at times marks us for inevitable rejection in the world, which may drive us into exile. But, in those times, his voice is often loudest, and we find him saying, *"...seek the Lord your God, and you will find him if you search for him with all your heart and all your soul"* (Deuteronomy 4:29). The isolation and rejection that Moses experienced was horrendous, and yet, in God's hands, it became the tool that shaped his character as a leader and prepared him for the destiny that God ordained. Both Moses and Jesus became well-acquainted with silence and solitude, accustomed to their own thoughts, alert to danger, and ready to hear and respond to God's voice. Only exile can impart these values to us, and they are precious gifts. For it is in such a state, undistracted by the clamour of the world, that we may cry into the abyss without inhibition. And in reply, the still small voice of God thunders.

A CRY INTO THE ABYSS

Growing up with solitude and silence my closest companions, I sensed some *Other* in the emptiness, whose presence eluded me on the playground, or when I was assaulted by media, but enfolded me when I was alone. I had no idea what this presence was. My parents and relatives never mentioned God during my childhood in the prairies, and yet he featured in a very dynamic, albeit ambiguous fashion, nonetheless. I have vague memories of interactions with this Other from an early age. I didn't know that I was praying, yet I have vivid recollections of asking for healing, for provision, for comfort, and for understanding. Even in the grip of occult deception and confusion during my teens, I instinctively cried out into the abyss, desperate to connect with the presence that I knew must be there, somewhere.

Childhood abuse at the hands of others may have left me wounded and damaged, yet in retrospect I wonder if perhaps the vulnerability that resulted led me to accept, unhesitatingly, the truth of the gospel when I finally heard it at the age of sixteen. My older brother had heard the gospel from a fellow student in university, while taking a class in astronomy. This student had become convinced of the existence of a Creator simply by gazing at the infinitely complex patterns in the universe. My brother accepted Jesus as Lord of his life and began to study the Bible for himself. As I had always looked up to him, I quickly noticed that he was becoming secretive, arriving home only to rush to his room with a mysterious black book tucked under his arm. I knocked on his door, demanding to know what was going on, but he put me off with platitudes. I know now that he simply needed his own time in exile to process the enormous change he was experiencing. But, eventually, he opened the door to me one night and explained his new beliefs. I was more than ready to hear his assertion that this Presence I yearned for did in fact exist. As with the saying attributed to Helen Keller, I declared, "I always knew He was there; but I didn't know His name." The change was immediate and dramatic. I no longer cried into the abyss; I spoke with its Master.

As I had absolutely no knowledge of either scripture or church tradition, I had no preconceptions as to what a new Christian was meant to do or experience. I began with the Gospel of John and moved on to the book of Acts. There I read that the experience of the supernatural was normative, and had no reason to believe otherwise. I renounced all occult practises and placed my spirituality in the hands of God, and of his son Jesus. I had no expectation that the experiential would cease, and so it did not. However, there was a distinct alteration; my dreams no longer forecast deaths or other negative events, and instead became a land of vivid but gentle metaphor, where God communicated biblical truth to me in story and symbol. Much later, I was delighted to discover these symbolic portrayals of truth presented in his Word. It was in a dream that I saw the white horse with its bloody mouth, ridden thunderously down from heaven towards a complacent, unfaithful bride. Much later I recognized Jesus in this image, as I read the book of Revelation. Likewise, I saw the city without walls, with source-less, life-giving water flowing from its centre long before I read of it in Zechariah and Revelation. Far from becoming dry and mundane, my subjective experiences increased and were vivid and rich, leading always to a deeper understanding of God's holiness and love.

I attended an inter-denominational church in Winnipeg while completing my last year of high school, hopeful that my isolation would finally end. To my alarm, I found that it did not. The Christianity of my peers was jarringly different from my own. Most had grown up in church, and the fluid ease with which they moved in the ecclesial culture intimidated me. I had found the One in whose presence no shadow could abide, and when I was with him in prayer, study, and worship, I was complete. But in church? Not so much.

I continued to have issues with social awkwardness and its resultant sense of isolation for many years. I fought it, knowing that I still had to find a way to live in my own hometown and play nice in this new, Christian sandbox. By then, unfortunately, I had a reputation for an off-putting intensity and general weirdness. Like Moses, I didn't seem to fit anywhere, trying to integrate into a community that did not always "get" me, nor I them. Yet I also knew that, like Moses, God was calling me to identify with these other believers, whether they "got" me or not.

I banked on Moses's example. Somehow, I would become the person God intended me to be, regardless of the acceptance or rejection of others. But this was not easy for me, as I craved the affirmation of those around me who defined "normal." And while the Christian community didn't overtly criticize me, neither did it offer any particular praise. My efforts only made things worse, as it became more obvious that I was on the fringes of that normality. I wavered between agonizing over social subtleties that I couldn't master and giving in to resentment, cynicism, and despair. I knew that God desired for me to identify with his people, but the path to belonging was lined with mirrors that only served to accentuate differences. How could I grow into the identity God had for me? How could I become one with other Christians? How could I survive this sense of isolation without being overcome by sorrow?

Faced with these questions, I looked to the Man of Sorrows himself.

MAN OF SORROWS

He was despised and rejected by men, a man of sorrows and acquainted with grief; and as one from whom men hide their faces he was despised, and we esteemed him not. (Isaiah 53:3, ESV)

For Moses, the journey to owning his identity as Deliverer of Israel was circuitous, plagued by criticism, set-backs, and self-doubt. But he got there, in the end. As a typology of the Saviour, Moses exemplified both perseverance and vulnerability. Likewise, when Jesus claimed his identity as Deliverer of the world, he did so despite the jeers and slander of his peers, despite the bloody sweat of Gethsemane, and despite the ignominy of his short career. Far from being dissuaded by sorrow, it seemed to give him an even greater sense of purpose. But it was a genuine sorrow, nonetheless.

Jesus had little regard for the approval or affirmation of others. Yet, while rejection and contempt may not have precipitated a crisis of identity, the prophecy from Isaiah implies that Jesus still felt pain and sorrow because of it. The rejection he experienced was not only from detached observers or offended political and religious parties, it was also deeply personal. We can imagine the pain he might have felt in being so grievously misunderstood, misjudged, and criticized by those closest to him, including his own family. Mark gives us a glimpse into what may have been a particularly cutting episode of rejection for Jesus, as his own mother and siblings become convinced that he is mentally ill and needs to be rescued from his own madness. Jesus, in the previous chapter, had been audaciously forgiving sins and claiming to be the "Lord of the Sabbath":

Then Jesus entered a house, and again a crowd gathered, so that he and his disciples were not even able to eat. When his family heard about this, they went to take charge of him, for they said, "He is out of his mind." (Mark 3:20)

Christ's earthly family may not have intended for their reaction to dismiss his claims to divinity, yet their attitude and words could not fail to sting. Which of us would not be wounded by our family shaking their heads over how we choose to define ourselves? If my son David had been ridiculed for his image of himself as "hot stuff on ice," he would have been crushed. Broken in spirit, he might never have gone on to become a valuable player. Jesus had an image of himself as God incarnate; his brothers were convinced that he was, at best, sleep-deprived and deluded. At worst, he was a nut-bar.

They were out to rescue not just their misguided relative, but to rescue their own reputation. Jesus was becoming an embarrassment to his family. It's easy to guess that Jesus knew the effect he was having on his relatives. Perhaps he even had them in mind when he called the crowd together and, in the context of claiming to be anointed by the Holy Spirit, declared that *"If a house is divided against itself, that house cannot stand"* (Mark 3:25). His own nuclear family, his "house," was at that moment divided and unstable. They needed to unite in their understanding of Jesus's identity, or they would fall.

The worried family sent someone to call for Jesus, presumably so they could take him home and rescue him from a situation that was getting out of hand. But Jesus stunned them with his response: *"'Who are my mother and my brothers?' he asked. Then he looked at those seated in a circle around him and said, 'Here are my mother and my brothers! Whoever does God's will is my brother and sister and mother'"* (Mark 3:33–35). Jesus, in the face of their rejection of his divine identity, turned the tables by rejecting the identity that this earthly family placed upon him. He was not theirs to correct or claim. Christ's response communicated that he knew exactly who he was, and what he was sent to do. Much as Moses chose to identify with the Hebrew slaves, rejecting his Egyptian family, Jesus broke away completely from his identity as the carpenter's son. The crowds were confused, angry, and skeptical:

> *"Where did this man get these things?" they asked. "What's this wisdom that has been given him? What are these remarkable miracles he is performing? Isn't this the carpenter? Isn't this Mary's son and the brother of James, Joseph, Judas and Simon? Aren't his sisters here with us?" And they took offence at him. Jesus said to them, "A prophet is not without honour except in his own town, among his relatives and in his own home."* (Mark 6:2–4)

Jesus broke away from any and all identities that either the Jews or Gentiles sought to thrust upon him. Rejection was inevitable. But he was the Man of Sorrows, acquainted with such grief, and it did not deter him. Astounding them with his teaching, confounding them with his power over disease, demons, and death, Christ rejected the mantle of mere manhood and boldly manifested the messianic. The result? Still more rejection.

Rejected now by his own family and local community, Jesus walked away from his hometown, amazed at their lack of faith. By now those in authority were furious: "*Some of them were looking for a reason to accuse Jesus, so they watched him closely to see if he would heal him on the Sabbath... Then the Pharisees went out and began to plot with the Herodians how they might kill Jesus*" (Mark 3:2, 6). They began to desperately search for some way to trap him, expose his identity as false, and find a legitimate justification for arresting him and putting him to death. By voluntarily rejecting the identity that his family imposed upon him, and then being rejected by both his own people and the authorities of the day, Jesus, like Moses, was now a "stranger in a strange land." This is reflected by his poignant words, "*...Foxes have dens and birds have nests, but the Son of Man has no place to lay his head*" (Matthew 8:20). The Saviour was in exile. Yet this earthly exile was not decreed as a punishment, but as a preparation for what lay ahead.

Exile crafts our identity like nothing else can if we are willing to surrender our sorrows to God and keep the chip off our shoulder.

LA GRINGA

After three non-stop days travelling by bus, I was groggy and disoriented. Was this Mexico? Who were these people, what were they saying?

"Vamanos, mija," the woman smiled, gently leading me by the arm to a waiting taxi. "Te vamos a llevar a la casa. We will take you home." I understood nothing of what they were saying, as it was all in Spanish. But I stumbled along, following their lead.

"Um, gracias," I mumbled, aware that I was probably being inexcusably rude. I should have shaken their hands, found the appropriate greetings in my phrase book, at the very least smiled and introduced myself. But at that moment I could not have cared less; they could be axe murderers leading me to a dark, bloody death. At least I would be able to lie down and close my eyes.

During the night I awoke, confused. Where was I? More importantly, where was the bathroom? Flicking on the bedroom light switch, I shrieked as a wave of enormous cockroaches scurried across the floor and disappeared into the wooden door frame. The senora and her children appeared instantly, but I swatted away her consoling hand in my panic and disgust. Her son Miguel took instant offence at my discourtesy.

"Mama!" he said angrily. "This gringa should not be here if she cannot be respectful!"

"Calmate, mijo," the lady shook her head; "She knows nothing of our ways. Right now, she is la Gringa, the stranger. But soon she will be your sister, tu hermana. Before one can learn a new name, one must forget the old one."

From her tone, I knew that she had already forgiven me my social faux pas. Her patience and tolerance was due, I saw, to the fact that she expected little better from an outsider.

Suddenly I smiled. I had, at last, found a place where a misfit could be accepted.

***

After graduating from high school, I decided, on what seemed a whim at the time, to sign up for a month-long cultural immersion program offered through the University of Winnipeg, travelling far into the interior of Mexico. I had never heard of the small, obscure state of Colima, and I spoke no Spanish whatsoever. This didn't dissuade me; I had lived for so long as a social "misfit" that I didn't fear it catching me unprepared. What did catch me by surprise was how much I enjoyed the cultural displacement itself. I felt like I had finally been given a valid, justifiable reason for being awkward. After all, I didn't just *feel* like an outsider in Colima, I actually *was* an outsider.

As a foreigner, I was *La Gringa*. Awkwardness was expected of me, and any social ineptness was graciously overlooked. When the month ended, I was so enamoured of the acceptance I felt there that I returned only briefly to Canada, working long enough to earn the money needed for an extended stay back in Colima. In all, I lived in Colima for almost six years, volunteering at a local orphanage and eventually becoming proficient enough in the language to enrol in a local Fine Arts Institute. The years were fulfilling to my artistic temperament, allowing me to perform regularly and travel extensively across Mexico, seeing places that tourists seldom frequented. I continued to volunteer and teach English and the Bible to the orphans, and they taught Spanish idioms to me. Over time I spoke, ate, acted, and lived more and more as a native Mexican.

Yet ironically, the more I adapted to the culture, the more uncomfortable I grew. As I became more linguistically and culturally fluent, the social bar was raised. I was now expected to understand and practice all the various social nuances of the Latino culture. It was assumed that I would be comfortable and at home in the kitchen with other women, when in fact I didn't have the slightest expertise or inclination in that regard. My lack of sensitivity to social cues was no longer tolerated; I should know better than to interrupt when a man is speaking. Suitors came my way, and my friends and neighbours were appalled that I showed no interest, as I was too old (by Latin standards) to remain single. Rumours began to circulate that I was lesbian—laughable at first, then hurtful. I was too tall, too assertive, too critical, too unfeminine to be "one of the girls." As a Christian, I was already suspect, viewed as a borderline heretic and cult member by the predominantly Catholic culture. I began to lose the credibility I fought so hard to attain, as I no longer met the higher expectations my integration into society would suggest.

My heart sank when I found that I was again just as much of a misfit in this culture as I had been in my own. The Mexican people were still gracious and forgiving, but held me at a distance, and I had few friends. I returned to Canada every six months, thinking I would find emotional reprieve, only to realize that I was so comfortable in the Latino world I no longer seemed to belong in my own country. I was offended by the unapologetic materialism and the focus on "First World problems," and found my North American peers unfriendly compared to the warmth and hospitality I had experienced in Mexico. My attempts at meaningful conversations were greeted with suspicion; how dare I invade their personal space with intimate queries? In Mexico I was "*La Gringa*," no matter how hard I tried. In Canada I had become "*La Mexicana*." I no longer fit in either country. Culturally, relationally, I had "no place to lay my head." I was an exile. Then I found another exiled soul and married him.

Marrying the son of ex-missionaries did not alleviate the loneliness that came with being socially awkward, but at least now we two misfits had one another. We had much in common. We felt like we were always on the outside of some secret inner circle whose handshake we could never quite master. As a couple, we continued to have a close connection with immigrants from Spanish-speaking cultures, even facilitating a support group for recent Latin American immigrants. Yet we never quite belonged in either the Western or Latino context, joking that we were like a plaid chameleon, able to change our colours to match each environment, but unable to cover up the jarring pattern of our differences.

Who was I? I still had no idea. Where did I belong? Nowhere, it seemed. Wherever I lived, I was an outsider. In this extended exile, my longing to belong grew overwhelming. I wanted to be on a team, to share inside jokes and idioms and history and purpose and T-shirts with matching logos. I wanted to belong to a people. But *which* people? Canadian? Christian? Latino? Which group, if any, should I identify with, and why was it so hard? When would I belong?

I was like Moses in Midian. I did not yet know that before I could belong, I must be sent. And in order to be sent, I would need to encounter the Sender.

CHAPTER EIGHT
Who Sends Me?

There the angel of the Lord appeared to him in flames of fire from within a bush. Moses saw that though the bush was on fire it did not burn up. So Moses thought, "I will go over and see this strange sight—why the bush does not burn up." When the Lord saw that he had gone over to look, God called to him from within the bush, "Moses! Moses!" And Moses said, "Here I am." "Do not come any closer," God said. "Take off your sandals, for the place where you are standing is holy ground." Then he said, "I am the God of your father, the God of Abraham, the God of Isaac and the God of Jacob." At this, Moses hid his face, because he was afraid to look at God. (Exodus 3:2–6)

Warning Moses that the ground he stands upon is holy, God speaks an astonishing affirmation of ancestry and identity to an abandoned, adopted, rejected, and confused old man, naming Moses in such a manner as to root him firmly in an impressive lineage of names: his father, Amram, Abraham, Isaac, and Jacob. Moses is named here in a way that could not fail to move him. He is reminded not just *who* he is, but *whose* he is. He is the son of his birth father, who was himself a son of the Hebrew patriarchs, and therefore is a descendent of those who belong to this God. Moses, who belonged to no one, is told that he is *one who belongs to God*, as did his father, and forefathers before him.

Did the mists of identity confusion begin to recede? Did Moses reflect, recalling that he has his mother's eyes, his father's nose, his great-great-great-grandfather's God? Moses is being clearly reminded that he does in fact belong to a people, one specific and unique people, coming from a long line of those who worshipped Yahweh. Moses has a place to perch on his own branch of the family tree. We could suppose that this would be enough.

THE FAMILY TREE

All our children showed an intense interest in their family heritage. They would pour over old photo albums and demand to know who these strangers were in relationship to themselves. They seemed to have a voracious appetite for a sense of extended family, and each loved to be told, "You have grandfather Warde's nose," or "You have your Ukrainian great-grandmother's hooded eyes," or "your British great-grandmother's cheekbones," etc. A passion for family history shows a desire to know not just who we are, but *whose* we are. At some deep level, we intuitively grasp that identity requires that we "belong" to someone, somewhere.

Our kids sought out this sense of belonging through researching our family tree, and even inventing a few branches of their own. At some point they fell under the impression that we had Spanish or Latin American blood somewhere in our family history, likely due to the fact that I was fluent in Spanish, and their father was born in Bolivia. Apparently they missed a few of the details, such as the fact that my husband had been born to missionary parents from England and Nova Scotia respectively, and that I, their mother, was a mutt daughter of second generation Scottish and Ukrainian immigrants who just happened to enjoy salsa.

Then we found out that somewhere, someone on my father's side had taken a Métis bride. My children were exactly one sixty-fourth part Cree. Over the next few years, this identity began to gain traction with our family because it fit with who we already sensed ourselves to be. It fit very well with our boy's innate love of the outdoors: fishing, hunting, camping. A consideration of our First Nations roots also affirmed and sharpened our daughter's already keen passion for social justice, birthing in her a desire to rewrite those school textbooks that did not adequately reflect the suffering of Indigenous peoples at the hands of settlers in North America. And knowing that my great-great-great immigrant grandfather had taken a Métis bride for the choice of the hundred dollars or hundred acres that the government offered along with her increased my own fervour for human rights in general and women's rights in particular.

These are just examples of small ways in which identity can be affirmed and shaped by knowledge of our roots. It both gives answers and raises questions about how identity can be both inherited and yet chosen. Identity is an unfolding of sorts; it takes time for each of us to grow into our own skin, to become comfortable accepting roles that reflect our identities. It also takes courage. At first, we may flounder at life's challenges, wondering if we are enough. We ask, "Am I ready for this? Is this really me?" Like Moses, we may hear the call, but our self-doubts respond, "Who, *me?*"

WHO, ME?

The Lord said, "I have indeed seen the misery of my people in Egypt. I have heard them crying out because of their slave drivers, and I am concerned about their suffering. So I have come down to rescue them from the hand of the Egyptians and to bring them up out of that land into a good and spacious land, a land flowing with milk and honey—the home of the Canaanites, Hittites, Amorites, Perizzites, Hivites and Jebusites. And now the cry of the Israelites has reached me, and I have seen the way the Egyptians are oppressing them. So now, go. I am sending you to Pharaoh to bring my people the Israelites out of Egypt." (Exodus 3:7–10)

Standing there before the burning bush, Moses is told that he is to be, at long last, the heroic deliverer he once hoped to be. God tells Moses that he is being sent back to the very people that had rejected him, so many years before. It should have been a dream come true for him; instead, he is plagued by self-doubt. "Who, me?" he wonders.

Long gone were the days when Moses might have considered himself a Deliverer; now, he is a simple sheep-herder. But the calling is clear: both a command to "go" and an assurance of being "sent" to deliver God's people from their oppressor. That Moses still struggles to grasp the implications of his sent-ness is evident, as he immediately mounts five consecutive objections. "*Who am I,*" he asks, "*that I should go to Pharaoh and bring the Israelites out of Egypt?*" (Exodus 3:11) This is surely the question that Moses has asked himself all his life. *Who am I?* Is it enough to belong to the lineage of Abraham, Isaac, and Jacob? Could that identity alone qualify him to be sent to this people, to become the hero he had once longed to be?

Who am I? In essence, Moses is here repeating the very question that was flung at him from the scornful Hebrew slaves he once sought to help, when they asked, "Who do you think you *are?*" He was no one, nothing. Surely this God in the burning bush made a mistake and confused him with someone else. Who did this God think that he, Moses, actually *was?* God's answer to Moses further establishes his identity through a clear, concise affirmation of relationship: "*And God said, 'I will be <u>with</u> you. And this will be the sign to you that <u>it is I who have sent you</u>: When you have brought the people out of Egypt, you will worship God on this mountain'*" (Exodus 3:12, emphasis mine).

First, God tells Moses *whose* he is: one of God's chosen people, a descendent of Abraham, Isaac, Jacob, through the lineage of his own biological father Amram; Moses is one of a people. As self-doubts persist, God then reminds Moses that he is also one whom God is *with.* Suddenly Moses is given both the roots and relationship which will define him. He is one whom God is *with,* and he is one whom God has *sent.* God affirms Moses's identity by establishing his past, his present, and his future. Moses has a past; he is an Israelite. He has a present; God is with him. And he has a future; he is one whom God is sending.

Thus defined, Moses goes from being the outcast of three Middle Eastern cultures to being the uniquely qualified founder of a divinely-designed culture in a distant land. The exile is not a punishment; God never intended for Moses to find roots in any one earthly culture, nor to cling to any identity other than that of being from, with, and sent—by God alone. The life events, orchestrated by God's hand, that systematically stripped Moses of any earthly identity, left him face-to-face with a God who now defines his sense of Self. Time and again, throughout the next forty years of his life, Moses comes back to the irrefutable truth of both belonging to God's people and being sent by God. It becomes, as it should for all Christ-followers, the solid rock foundation of identity. Without this, our house indeed is built upon sinking sand. And storms are sure to come.

NOMASAYIN'?

"Who's there?"

I was being followed. As I walked through the vacant building, I was sure that I could hear the echo of footsteps behind me. I froze, glancing around anxiously, but I could see no one hiding in the shadows. Perhaps it was my imagination.

With a heavy, solemn step I continued on with my task. I paused at each door, switching off the lights with a sigh and closing each door behind me with a hollow clang. Where once the building had been full of music and laughter, now there was an accusing silence. We had killed the church. Grief hung on me like a heavy shroud, making it difficult to raise my arm as I locked up.

There it was again. I stopped and, over the pounding of my own pulse, I heard it again. Footsteps behind me, a rhythmic shuffling that ceased almost immediately. There was someone there. I had to see, had to face whatever was there.

But in that odd paralysis that occurs in dreams, I was unable to fully turn my head. In that instant, I realized that I was asleep, and my racing heart slowed. I had imagined the danger. But why couldn't I turn my head? The shuffling noise began again, and I tried to crane my neck, to no avail. Then, suddenly I heard a soft voice, crooning what sounded like a strain of rap lyrics.

"Oh yeah!" I heard fingers, hands, and toes. Snap, clap, snap, tap. The voice seemed to come from some point a metre or more above the back of my head. Whatever this thing was, it was huge!

The voice went on. "Mm hmm, yeah, lez go. Nomasayin'? Lez do it, yo. So, where we goin'? Lez go, lez go!"

What on Earth…?

Suddenly, I caught a glimpse from my peripheral vision, and what I saw was enough to stop my heart. Looming well over fourteen feet tall and bouncing happily on the balls of his enormous feet was an angel. He was huge, dark-skinned, grinning and clapping his enormous hands together eagerly, moving to some funky strain of celestial music that only he could hear. With dream-like certainty, I knew that this angel had a name, as with the angels mentioned in the book of Revelations. He was the angel who named himself after our own church. His enthusiasm appalled me.

We had just shut down the church! How could he possibly be so happy? And yet clearly he was eagerly anticipating our next move and looking forward to where he, the essence of all that was good and true about our previous church, would next be sent.

And we—war-torn, reluctant, bruised, and fearful—were being sent along with him.

***

For twelve years, my family was a part of what eventually became an in-grown and unhealthy church community, full of as-yet undisclosed sin at the leadership level. With deep sorrow, our leadership team finally gathered and agreed that it was time to shut the church down. It was a horribly painful time. Many of us felt like lost sheep, floundering and without clear direction as to what to do next. What would we do? Where would we go? Should we find another church within the same denomination and stagger on?

The abysmal state of our family dynamics, with our eldest in full-blown rebellion, dissuaded us from a lateral move within the denomination. We needed something else, but we weren't sure exactly what. Together, my husband and I took stock of our relational resources, assessed our strengths, and exposed our weaknesses. In raw self-examination we came to the conclusion that we had—as a family, as well as a church—become self-centred, critical isolationists. We had even come to take pride in our own isolation, a secretly-seething "remnant" of disgruntled Charismatics surrounded by the dead religiosity of all other ecclesial streams. We had never considered going to any other kind of church, convinced as we had been that there was nothing they could teach us. Or was there? One glance at our family was now enough to convince us otherwise. We were in trouble, and we needed help. And so, we joined a large, traditional evangelical church, with hopes that we would somehow absorb missing social skills and integrate into the mainstream majority that we'd always disdained. We were secretly terrified. The transition was brutal; the memories of our first Sunday, which I related earlier, still make me wince. They were all so... *nice.*

I felt like a clumsy and uncouth boor in a society of solicitous sophisticates. They all knew what to do with their hands; mine twitched without a guitar pick or a book. They were skilled in the art of evasive non-threatening conversation. "Well, that's an interesting thought. Thank you for sharing!" They had carefully acquiescent answers to potentially touchy questions. "Well, that's an interesting question. What do *you* think?"

Where did they learn all these social graces? How on Earth did they stay so calm, so nonreactive? I was a tumultuous storm of opinions, obsessions, over-reactive tendencies, and a smattering of other ADD traits. I felt envious and insecure. How would I know where the friendliness ended and real friendship began? Were they just tolerating me, or did any of them actually like me? I did not want careful friendliness, I wanted friends. Adrift in this sea of "Seeker-Sensitives," I found myself becoming a combative "Sensor–Seekative." Where were the prophets who would get in my face, confront my selfishness, provoke my passion for God, challenge my complacency? How could we ever have thought that God was sending us to this church, how could we ever belong to this people? Why had we come here? It was a miserable, uncomfortable time, like wearing the wrong size shoes and desperately waiting for them to break in.

THE CHURCH OF THE BORG

It took time for us to settle into the new church, years to lose the chip on our shoulder: that self-fulfilling expectation of rejection. There were walls to hit, egos to deflate. I had, in the course of a dysfunctional heathen childhood and lop-sided Christian youth, acquired none of the skills that might allow me to integrate seamlessly into such gracious society. I couldn't read subtle social clues and had never been mentored in the art of small-talk or entertaining others in my home. I failed miserably as an Alpha Table Leader (I tended to actually answer questions, rather than reflect them back). I had no generational Christian roots to look back on, no personal history of Oma and Opa dodging bullets in the old country, no extended family of believers that had taught me to cook, bake, sew, or avoid inflicting my innate self-absorption upon others. I had no patience for protocol, minimal interest in small children, a horror of all crafts, and I had never listened to a local Christian radio station or owned a purse.

Instead, I had a sharp tongue, an invasive conversational approach, a tendency to weep messily during worship, and—metaphorically speaking—large feet that managed to tread on nearby toes while still remaining firmly embedded in my mouth. A misfit. How could these nice people ever fit me in to their church? Still, with Borg-like determination, church leadership worked to bring us into the fold. "You will be assimilated. Resistance is futile." A promise? A threat? At the time, I wasn't sure.

Work. Surely that was the key. To immerse ourselves in the busy fellowship of functionality. Perhaps we would find relational fulfillment by signing up for as many events and volunteer ministries as we could. For a time, it seemed to be helping, and we felt a sense of "trench" brotherhood as we laboured side by side with relative strangers in various church contexts. But then our family crisis with John hit us hard, and we were suddenly knocked out of commission. It was a time of both discovery and of disappointment. For, although a few people emerged at that time as genuine, deep friends, much of the relational closeness that I'd been experiencing up to that point evaporated. I realized that most of my relationships did not have any foundation outside of the context of service. I had precious few agenda-free friendships where one is sought after simply for the pleasure of enjoying each other's company. Instead, I had become the blind woman at the quilting bee:

an uncomfortable, somewhat useless presence to be pitied and thrown the occasional conversational bone.

To be fair, some of my friends offered me manageable tasks out of genuine compassion, in an effort to restore my sense of significance and belonging. To my shame, I snarled at them, feeling patronized. I did not want to be "kept busy," thank you very much. I wanted someone to weep with me, to hurt at my hurt. Yet, even while I seethed at the normality in which I was unable to participate, I was still convinced that we were meant to be at this church. Surely, we had been sent to this people, if big Black angel rappers can in fact be trusted. I just could not for the life of me figure out why! Had we been sent to be agents of change in this church, or to be changed ourselves? The answer was: both. The ones to whom God had sent us were about to become the ones who would, in turn, send us.

THE SENT ONES

"So, is this, like, a punishment?" John asked, looking at the tickets.
"I mean, it's been a while since I blew anything up, so..."

"No, idiot!" I replied, exasperated. "It's called a family vacation. Lots of nice, happy, normal families take them."

"Are there bugs? I hate bugs." Robin shook her head vehemently. "If there are going to be bugs, then count me out."

"Seriously?" David rolled his eyes. "It's Mexico! They breed bugs there for sport. There are like these cockroach Olympics or something."

Undeterred, my husband pulled the travel knapsacks down from the attic and blew off the dust and cobwebs. We were taking a vacation, darn it. We were going to vacate, good and proper.

As our new church helped to set a new standard for normalcy in our lives, we had achieved a precarious balance of emotional health and well-being: busyness with intimacy, breadth of service with depth of ministry, strong opinions with, we hoped, more teachable spirits. The stresses of the previous years had not allowed us to enjoy being together as a family, and we needed something to jump start that process again. I had announced to the children that we would be going down to the city in Mexico where I once lived, studied, and worked when I was their age. No astonished applause greeted this announcement. Bugs, dysentery, heat rash, active volcanoes, drug cartels, and potential alien invasion were all offered as objections; I refused to be dissuaded from my dream.

That Sunday, the pastor of our church—having a strongly missional focus—invited us to present our plans from the stage. I was embarrassed, but my husband and I complied, while our kids cringed in the back row. This was hardly an outreach trip, I protested. It was merely a reluctant family holiday. We'd agreed to visit our MB Mission national representatives in Guadalajara while we were there, but it wasn't like we were being sent on any mission. The pastor corrected me gently, firmly, and publicly.

"Wherever we go, Nikki, is where we have been sent. That's who we are."

***

With those words, another piece of the puzzle fell into place. Our mission-minded church had reminded us that being sent was not an event, but an all-encompassing way of life. Being sent is our primary identity: we are the Sent Ones. Christ ensured that our mandate and commission was unforgettably clear; Matthew 28:18–20 leaves no wiggle room. His final command was not situational, but eternal in scope, an identity to be lived out until the end of the age. Jesus, at the completion of his mission on Earth, spoke these final words over his friends:

…"All authority in heaven and on earth has been given to me. Therefore go and make disciples of all nations, baptizing them in the name of the Father and of the Son and of the Holy Spirit, and teaching them to obey everything I have commanded you. And surely I am with you always, to the very end of the age."

We are, as Christians, the *Sent Ones*. The Greek word *apostolos* means a "delegate, messenger, one sent forth with orders." The Great Commission was not the Great Suggestion, it was a command. A central tenet of our identity as *Sent Ones* is the clear understanding that Christ intends for us to focus not on Self, but on Other. We must go well beyond the mere promptings of social conscience to an incarnational humanism that flows from the very presence of Christ, who lived a life of radical other-mindedness and invites us to be shaped in his image. Standing on the stage in church that Sunday, the enormity of this identity overwhelmed me, and in a flash I suddenly understood why I could never feel completely at home in any one culture. When I was in Canada, I was being *sent* to Canadians. When in Colima, I was *sent* to the Mexicans. I was both *of* them and yet *apart* from them. Never the citizen, ever the envoy. I was *sent*. I was one of the *Sent Ones* of God. With the entire congregation adding their "amen," the pastor prayed over our family, and sent us off the stage, full of a new peace and confidence. This would not be just any old family vacation!

Jesus, in sending his followers, breathes out a blessing of peace upon those who will receive it. In John 20:21, he says, "*Peace be with you! As the Father has sent me, I am sending you.*'" That peace is still there for us all; it is not always instantaneous, nor does it go unchallenged, but it is based in the unshakable reality that he is with us "*always, to the very end of the age.*" In sending us, Jesus also imparts us with authority. This is, perhaps, harder to comprehend. When the leadership laid hands on us, sending us off to Colima, I admit I had doubts our shaky, dysfunctional family would see any of the "mighty and wonderful works" they prayed for. Amazingly, that semi-vacation was riddled with miraculous, divine appointments that had far-reaching and lasting effects both in Colima, our church, and our own lives. We were to meet and become lasting friends with a man who would eventually become the president of the MB conference in Mexico. In sending us, Jesus imparted true authority to us to minister powerfully to the ones to whom we were being sent.

The Kingdom of God has a chain of command, and we are a part of it. It is because of the absolute nature of Christ's own authority that he is able to invest authority in us, as John 16:15 says, "*All that belongs to the Father is mine. That is why I said the Spirit will receive from me what he will make known to you*" (emphasis mine). And Luke 10:16 tells us that "*Whoever listens to you listens to me; whoever rejects you rejects me; but whoever rejects me rejects him who sent me."* Here is a chain of command where *exthusia*—the authorized power of God—is given to us to use in his name. When a father adds his son's name to his own Visa account, that child is then authorized to use that card, even though it's not his own credit card. We have had our names added to Christ's account.

With authority comes a certain power when we humbly ask for and receive the anointing of the Holy Spirit to empower us in our sent-ness. This power (Greek: *dýnamis*) imparts to us, as it did to those gathered at Pentecost, the resources and abilities required to wield our authority properly. We are human, and there is potential for abuse of both power and authority; lamentably, the Church throughout history has seen its share of both. Many of us are gun-shy, having been the victims ourselves of abusive authority. We question whether we should use the gifts of the Spirit at all, we doubt that we have been sent anywhere, and we demand infallible proof of God's plan before we will move a single step.

Sound familiar? It describes most of us. It certainly describes Moses.

SAYS WHO?

In what is perhaps a projection of his own insecurity, Moses questions God. How could he be sure that the one sending him would back him up? What assurance did Moses have that he had any authority at all with his own people, much less with Pharaoh? Moses is, in effect, questioning God's credentials here and, amazingly, God does not seem the least offended by this. Moses asks, *"Suppose I go to the Israelites and say to them, 'The God of your fathers has sent me to you,' and they ask me, 'What is his name?' Then what shall I tell them?"* (Exodus 3:13). Despite knowing that he belongs to the lineage of God's people, that God is *with* him and that he is being *sent,* Moses still doubts. Is this God really so powerful that an endorsement from him would have any weight? Could a voice from a burning bush really have any credibility?

God's response is a rebuff aimed directly at the core of Moses's self-doubts. *"'I am who I am. This is what you are to say to the Israelites: 'I am has sent me to you... This is my name forever, the name you shall call me from generation to generation'"* (Exodus 3:14–15). It's as if God were chiding Moses, saying "You are the one with the identity issue here,

Moses, not me. I know exactly who I am and have no need to prove it to you or anyone else." Yet Moses remains uncertain. What kind of an answer would that be to the Hebrews? A no-name God had sent him to deliver them from Egypt. Moses continues to dodge God's call with a series of "what if" scenarios in which God's authority, and that of Moses, is sure to be challenged.

WHAT IF...?

Once burned, twice shy. Moses once attempted to lead the Hebrews and it did not go well. Now he asks God, *"What if they do not believe me or listen to me and say, 'The Lord did not appear to you?'"* (Exodus 4:1). What guarantee could God give that Moses would not again be rejected, humiliated, and run out of town back into Midian? God's patience here with Moses is astounding. Knowing the wounds and traumas of his past, God does not (yet) rebuke Moses for his unbelief. Eighty years of confusion, rejection, and isolation have taken their toll. And so, God reassures Moses that, far from being humiliated, Moses will shock and silence the opposition with his authority and power by the signs God works through him: first, by turning Moses's staff into a snake and back, and second, by afflicting Moses's hand with leprosy and then healing it again. God finishes by saying that, if the Hebrews don't believe the first or second sign, Moses is to take some water from the Nile and pour it on the ground, where it will turn to blood.

The choice of a staff as a symbol of authority, and as the instrument through which God will work powerful signs and wonders, is significant. The two words for staff in Hebrew are *shevet* and *matteh*. Both words have a similar primary meaning of a "staff" or "rod," for example, as a shepherd's staff or as the sceptre of a ruler. The staff symbolizes authority, not just of an individual but of a united, cohesive organization. Both *shevet* and *matteh* are also used to describe the various tribes of the Jewish peoples, bound together by ties of kinship, history, and destiny. In Genesis 49:10, the patriarch Jacob calls his sons around his deathbed to pronounce blessings, warnings and prophecy. To Judah he says: *"The scepter will not depart from Judah, nor the ruler's staff from between his feet, until he to whom it belongs shall come and the obedience of the nations shall be his."* The word translated here as "sceptre" is the Hebrew *shevet,* which signifies a rod or staff of authoritative rule. As each tribe of Israel had its own rod or staff with the associated tribal identity, a dynamic equivalent would be, "This tribal identity and authority shall not depart from Judah..."

And so, when God asks Moses what is in his hand, Moses would know the symbolic meaning, he would reflect on his own history, identity, and purpose. Moses would understand that God was giving him authority to rule. Moses was from the *shevet,* or tribe, of Levi. Looking at the rod in his hand, Moses would know that in Hebrew it was a symbol not just of authority, but also of "belonging" to a people. God uses this powerful symbol, with its many conflicting emotional connotations for Moses, to unify the whole of his people. They would be as one tribe, and Moses would lead them. The Hebrews would know that God had sent Moses; there would be proof to back up the claim. God's commissioning of Moses was to be public, powerful, and irrefutable, just as it was with Jesus.

THE DOVE DESCENDS

The translator was clearly confused. What exactly was I trying to say?

"Ask him," I repeated slowly, "what his theological stance is on women in leadership. I am just curious," I added mildly, wanting to ensure that the pastor did not hear my question as a challenge.

Our team had been in Myanmar for almost a week now, travelling by foot and water buffalo-drawn carts from village to village, seeking to encourage the pockets of Christian believers that were facing persecution from Buddhist extremists in the countryside. I had just finished a lengthy time of conversation and prayer with the pastor of one village church, who happened to be a woman. I was wondering how this fit with the patriarchal nature of Burmese culture, which held that that men are born with "phon" (power, glory, holiness), but women are not. Now I had an opportunity to speak with our mission agency's national partner, also a pastor. Haltingly, the translator conveyed my question to him.

Understanding dawned in the pastor's eyes, and he threw back his head and laughed.

"This is—what is the phrase? This is an issue for another land, another time," he explained through our translator. "Here, now, we have very different issues."

The translator nodded at me with a smile. "I think he is saying that worrying about women in church leadership is a First World Problem."

Animated, the pastor continued to speak, gesticulating and pointing to the bamboo huts we were leaving behind. Then the translator turned to me to explain.

"In your world you worry about gender, about education, about many things. Before someone can lead your church they must be so perfect! Here," he waved his hand at the jungle that surrounded us, "our worry is to choose someone who has been free from the betel leaf long enough that the other believers will follow. It is also good if they have read some of the Bible."

"That's it?" I stuttered. "You let someone become a pastor as long as they are not still addicted to drugs?" Setting the bar a bit low, I thought, dismayed. Through the translator, the pastor responded with a shrug.

"That," he said, "and they must have healed and delivered at least a dozen people." He smiled at my wide eyes. "Then we know that God has chosen them to lead."

***

Sure of his sent-ness, the Saviour of humanity faced no crisis of identity. And yet, God still chose to commission him publicly and powerfully. Significantly, in the moment Christ publicly identifies with the sinners to whom he was sent, he receives God's public affirmation of who, and whose, he is in a powerful symbolic confirmation of his divinity and sovereignty. Fully embracing his mission, Jesus stands, vulnerable and exposed, in the waters of the Jordan River, waiting to be baptized for sins he had never, would never, commit. And, as he rises from the waters of that river, the Spirit descends *"like a dove,"* and a voice from heaven speaks, proclaiming Christ's true identity: "*...This is my Son, whom I love; with him I am well pleased*" (Matthew 3:17).

Who is Jesus? He is the beloved of the Father, one whom God is "with," just as God was with Moses. The prophecies confirm this: "*All this took place to fulfill what the Lord had said through the prophet: 'The virgin will conceive and give birth to a son, and they will call him Immanuel' (which means 'God with us')*" (Matthew 1:22–23). God calls him "my son," just as God affirmed the familial ties that defined Moses by assuring him, "*I am the God of your father...*" Jesus, like Moses, is one who belongs to God. And like Moses, Jesus is also a Sent One.

Christ has a clear grasp of his identity from the start, which we can see when, upon beginning his formal ministry on Earth, he presents himself in the synagogue of his hometown to offer that day's reading of the scripture. He reads from Isaiah 61:1–2:

> *The Spirit of the Lord is on me, because he has anointed me to proclaim good news to the poor.* He has sent me *to proclaim freedom for the prisoners and recovery of sight for the blind, to set the oppressed free, to proclaim the year of the Lord's favor...* (emphasis mine)

Mesmerized, the crowds wonder at the solemnity of his reading, and then are shocked to hear this town carpenter's son declare, "*Today this scripture is fulfilled in your hearing*" (Luke 4:21). Jesus knows that he is sent; knew it, in fact, before he ever left his heavenly abode. His Father God "*...so loved the world, that <u>he sent</u> his one and only Son, that whoever believes in him shall not perish, but have everlasting life*" (John 3:16, emphasis mine).

Jesus, like Moses, takes strength and authority from this sent-ness in times of trial. Both leaders have their identities severely challenged, forcing them time and again to choose to take their identity not from their roles, relationships, or ambitions, not from the opinions of others, but solely from God. The certainty of their calling is crucial to their survival as leaders. As their fame and renown grow, it becomes increasingly difficult to ignore the crowds, who criticize them relentlessly, whether from frustrated ambition, jealousy, or fear. "If you are who you say," they cry, "then do as we ask!"

We should not be surprised when accusations are flung; God-given identities will always come under attack. It can, however, come as a bit of a shock when that attack comes from God himself.

CHAPTER NINE
Remember Who You Are

"Delhi?" Amy's jaw dropped. "What happened to France?" Stunned, she leaned back in her chair.

"We sense that God wants you elsewhere," was the gentle but unapologetic reply from the mission agency representative. There was sympathy in the tone, but the words had an unyielding quality. Amy turned to her husband, near tears. This was all wrong. After all the months of discernment, all the training, all the financial sacrifices and all the time spent preparing their hearts for full-time mission work, suddenly their plan had changed.

"I was so ready. It took so long, and I was finally ready," Amy shook her head in bewilderment. They had quit their jobs, rented out their house, met and fallen in love with the Paris team, and imagined raising their three little girls speaking French as a first language. And now… Delhi? Smoggy, crowded, chaotic, hot, horrible Delhi?

Amy's husband Chris sought to reassure her. "This must be where God wants us." He held her hand and squeezed it lovingly. "We said we were giving up control of our lives to him, remember?"

"I remember!" Amy looked rueful. "I just didn't expect this!"

"We'll be okay," Chris told her.

They were not okay. Upon arrival in India a few months later, they were blasted by what was to become the worst heat wave to have hit the country in decades. With people literally dying on the street, Amy was trapped in their tiny bedroom, a prisoner of the small air-conditioner that bravely chugged night and day. The children longed to be outside, but their short forays into the street were a nightmare of humidity, killing temperatures, and the worst air quality on the planet. The team members they had come to join were unable to renew their visas and could not remain in the country, leaving them on their own. Their family was sick almost constantly, even to the point of one of their children being hospitalized.

While their relationship with God grew deeper and richer, there were times when it seemed as if he were impervious to their plight. Had the one they loved and trusted most in life, now become their enemy?

***

Like our missionary friends, it took some time to convince Moses to totally change the direction of his life. God was sending him back to the one place he had no desire to go: Egypt. It had been a hard sell to begin with, but Moses was finally won over; the voice from the burning bush eroded his doubts, calmed his fears, affirmed his identity, and equipped him with a miraculous staff to prove his credibility before all. Resolute, Moses went back to Midian, and, apparently, announced to his family that they were to begin packing. They were moving to Egypt. Together with his wife and sons, Moses heads out, seemingly confident of his calling and obeying God. Then, out of the blue, God attacks him. We read:

> *At a lodging place on the way, the Lord met Moses and was about to kill him. But Zipporah took a flint knife, cut off her son's foreskin and touched Moses' feet with it. "Surely you are a bridegroom of blood to me," she said. So the Lord let him alone. (At that time she said "bridegroom of blood," referring to circumcision).* (Exodus 4:24–26)

The passage is a bewildering one, and commentators suggest various explanations. Two things are, however, quite clear: Moses comes close to death and at least one of his sons has not been circumcised. The question is, why?

Circumcision was not widely practised in the Near East at that time, though both the Egyptians and the Hebrews had largely adopted it as a custom: Hebrews on the eighth day following birth, and Egyptians at age thirteen. The Old Testament first mentions the symbolic origin of Jewish circumcision in Genesis 17. It was to be a tangible sign of the covenant between God and Israel, applicable to all males in the house of Abraham; any male not circumcised would break that covenant and be "...cut off from his people" (Genesis 17:14).

Moses himself would have been circumcised before he was adopted by the Egyptian princess. Perhaps that's how she knew that the infant was a Hebrew in the first place. It's not clear if circumcision was practised by the Midianites, however. It's possible that Zipporah, daughter of the Midianite priest Jethro, and wife to Moses, may have found the custom distasteful. Whether to appease his wife, or to conform to the customs of the Midianites, Moses failed to circumcise at least one of his two sons. This was a serious omission in God's sight. Moses may have agreed to return to Egypt and be God's instrument of deliverance for Israel, but his failure to circumcise a son communicated a lack of follow-through. In attacking him, God was, in essence, warning Moses to take his own commitment more seriously, to remember who he was. Like my friends Chris and Amy, Moses agreed to give control of his life to God without realizing that God very much intended to take him at his word.

The rite of circumcision, initiated with Abraham, was to be for "... every male... including those born in your household or bought with money from a foreigner—those who are not your offspring" (Genesis 17:12). This symbol of commitment and submission was meant to be not just for one person, nor for a single nuclear family, but for a people in perpetuity. Circumcision was a sign of belonging, tangible evidence that a man was knit into the Hebrew community. God had taken time to affirm Moses in his identity as a descendent of Abraham, Isaac, and Jacob; threatening him with death underscores the seriousness of this familial tie. Moses could not ever again view himself as a free agent. He must remember who he is and take that identity seriously, applying it not just to himself but to all males born in his household, including the son that had escaped the knife. God attacks him on this issue, as if he were asking, "Will you claim your identity or not?" In that moment of confrontation, God makes it a life or death issue for Moses, because later, it will be a life or death issue for the entire Hebrew nation.

A MATTER OF LIFE AND DEATH

"Pass the potatoes, please."

Eyes blazing, Liz slammed the casserole down in front of her husband. Murray winced, embarrassed before their guests at the obvious discord. Squirming, I buried my nose in my dish and tried to ignore the brewing argument. It was not a new one.

"Is that all you can say?" Liz demanded of her husband. "You want me to feed you? Well I'm fed up, do you hear me? I am not going to that insipid church one more week."

"Now, now," Murray glanced my way. "This isn't the time, dear..."

"There is a never a good time," his wife spat out bitterly. "You never want to talk about how I feel. Just yanked us off the mission field for no good reason, and now you expect me to somehow become the sweet, domestic Canadian housewife. Well, it's not happening! These are not the ones that God sent me to! These are not my people!" Furious, she stormed from the dining room, leaving us in awkward silence.

The family had left their work in Papua New Guinea rather abruptly, some decades before, mostly due to the combative and antagonistic nature of Liz's interactions with other members of the mission team. She had never reconciled herself to leaving, and her constant complaints and negativity had taken a toll on their children, their marriage, and, more recently, Murray's mental health. He was frequently depressed and unable to sleep well.

"I wish," Murray sighed, laying down his fork, "That she could see Canada with the same missional eyes that she once saw New

Guinea. But she refuses to make friends, to involve herself in the local church in any way."

"I'm sorry, Murray." I began to clear the dishes. "Maybe with time?"

"It's been years. I don't know what it will take for her to realize that she is just as much a part of the Body of Christ here as ever we were in New Guinea. She's wrong, you know." Murray stood up and pushed in his chair. "Wherever the Church is, they are our people!"

***

It wasn't until another ten years had passed that Liz realized her wrongdoing. Pushed beyond the limits of his emotional endurance, Murray suffered a complete breakdown. There was a genuine risk that he might be a danger to himself and become suicidal. His wife's inability to forgive him, and her adamant refusal to identify herself with their local church context, had literally become a matter of life or death.

Liz was horrified by her husband's state and determined to avoid provoking another. She began to curb her tongue, which in turn allowed her heart to begin to heal. Murray's crisis compelled Liz towards greater involvement with their neighbourhood church, and slowly the aging couple built a network of genuine friends and a fruitful ministry. It's very likely that this saved Murray's life.

Israel's allegiance to corporate identity, shown through the tangible symbol of circumcision, later proved to be their only preservation from the Angel of Death that was to visit the Egyptians. Identity became a matter of life or death; God emphasizes this with his attack on Moses at this early juncture. What form did this threat to his life take? Whether it was an encounter with the Angel of the Lord—a theophany as with Jacob and the Angel of the Lord in Genesis 32—or a potentially fatal illness that struck Moses down, it seems that Zipporah understood exactly what was happening and why. Obviously upset, she seizes a sharp implement, either impulsively or perhaps because Moses is too ill to do so himself, and cuts off her son's foreskin. The tension is palpable, and, as Zipporah or their sons aren't mentioned again until Jethro brings them out to the desert to be reunited with Moses in Exodus 18, we may well wonder if she and Moses parted company after this incident. God made his point; Moses must take seriously his commitment to self-identify as one of the Hebrews.

More challenges were yet to come, as Moses set his face to return to Egypt and confront Pharaoh. But perhaps, having been confronted and challenged by God himself, Moses felt less hesitant to face the opposition of a mere mortal, even if that mortal was the ruling monarch of Egypt. But Moses was in for a shock. For it was not only Pharaoh who opposed him, but the Hebrews themselves, bitter and bent under their burden of bricks and straw.

BRICKS AND STRAW

Armed with an assurance of miraculous signs and wonders, and a more articulate mouthpiece in the person of his brother Aaron, Moses arrives in Egypt. How did he feel? Did he hope that his reputation as an escaped criminal died along with Pharaoh forty years earlier? Did he glance at his staff and wonder how he was going to get through to his people?

Moses assembles the Hebrews and presents himself as their *de facto* leader. At first, they're impressed by the signs, and they accept him. All goes well, until Moses approaches Pharaoh for the first time, and is utterly scorned. The ruler scoffs at his presumption, saying, "... *Who is the Lord, that I should obey him and let Israel go? I do not know the Lord and I will not let Israel go*" (Exodus 5:2). Moses has no credibility as yet with this ruler, and, as he is about to find out, precious little with his own people, despite the signs and wonders that follow.

It's easy to lead when things are going well. We can even remain confident in the face of opposition, so long as there is support from the team, as it were. Moses was expecting the rejection and scorn of Pharaoh and the Egyptians, but he was not expecting his own brethren to oppose him. Yet, that's precisely what happens. Even while he consistently demonstrates that God is indeed with him, besting Pharaoh in every encounter, Moses loses favour with the very people he is championing. They, it seems, were expecting quick deliverance. They were not themselves prepared for the opposition that God was allowing, and they blamed Moses when Pharaoh increased their workload instead of liberating them. The Hebrews lash out angrily against Moses, saying, "...*May the Lord look on you and judge you! You have made us obnoxious to Pharaoh and his officials and have put a sword in their hand to kill us*" (Exodus 5:21).

Not an auspicious beginning. But, to his credit, rather than strike back, Moses defers this complaint to its rightful owner:

> *Moses returned to the Lord and said, "Why, Lord, why have you brought trouble on this people? Is this why you sent me? Ever since I went to Pharaoh to speak in your name, he has brought trouble on this people, and you have not rescued your people at all."* (Exodus 5:22–23)

Rather than be defeated, Moses asserts his identity. God had spoken to him; he would darn well talk back. If God called him to deliver the Hebrews, then Moses would take the problems to God. Moses refuses to back down from his calling, despite the criticism and slander from his people. God's response is clear. Stay the course. The Lord instructs Moses to use this crisis as an opportunity to refresh the vision, to remind the Hebrews of who, and whose, they are, and of their new calling. They are a people who belong to God, who are being sent to take possession of a new land. God tells Moses:

> *Therefore, say to the Israelites: "I am the Lord, and I will bring you out from under the yoke of the Egyptians. I will free you from being slaves to them, and I will redeem you with an outstretched arm and with mighty acts of judgment. I will take you as my own people, and I will be your God. Then you will know that I am the Lord your God, who brought you out from under the yoke of the Egyptians. And I will bring you to the land I swore with uplifted hand to give to Abraham, to Isaac and to Jacob. I will give it to you as a possession. I am the Lord."* (Exodus 6:6–8)

Despite these assuring words, however, the people continue to gripe, as their yoke of slavery grows even heavier under Pharaoh's punishing hand. Time and again, Moses confronts the despot, demanding freedom for the Hebrews. Time and again, the result is even harsher bondage. The Hebrews cry out for Moses to stop, he was only making their lot worse. They are angry, critical, and ready to stone him. Pharaoh's heart continues to grow harder towards their plight. Ironically, we read that it is actually God who is responsible; he himself is hardening the heart of Pharaoh. How could this be?

Earlier, we recounted the tragic tale of the high priest Eli, who chose to abdicate the privilege and responsibility of his office in favour of lazy parenting and choice cuts of meat. God's rebuke to him, and to his self-indulgent sons, was to say, "*Those who honor me I will honor, but those who despise me will be disdained.*" The word "honour," we recall, is *kabed*, which can mean to "give weight to." This word is also found in Exodus. Here, it describes a process of heart-hardening, as Pharaoh's heart became resolute and firm in his negative attitude towards the Israelites. Literally, the phrase implies that Pharaoh "gave weight" or importance to the evil inclinations of his own heart, deliberately rejecting God's perspective of the Israelites as being a chosen people. Pharaoh did this repeatedly, by his own choice, in Exodus 8:15, 8:32, 9:34. And God not only allows Pharaoh to continually harden his heart, but *co-operates* with that process.

Exodus 7:3, 13, 9:12, 10:1, 20, 27, 11:10, and 14:4, 8 all speak of God as the one who hardens the heart of Pharaoh. The words used most in these verses are derivatives of the Hebrew *chazaq*, meaning "to strengthen, encourage, and establish." In Exodus 10:1 we read, "*Then the Lord said to Moses, 'Go to Pharaoh, for I have hardened his heart and the hearts of his officials...'*" Here again is the word *kabed*, meaning "heavy, weighty," fits well with our English expression "to give weight to," in the sense of honouring someone's preferences. God did not arbitrarily alter Pharaoh's heart to be set against the Hebrews. Rather, God "gave weight to" the already present murderous inclinations of this ruler's heart, sovereignly stepping back and allowing Pharaoh full reign to nurture and vent his hate.

By paying heed to his own sinful desires for so long, Pharaoh is no longer able to choose any other path. He has given weight to the wrong inclinations and is now trapped in his chosen identity of being the murderous and doomed persecutor of God's people. Why does God allow this? Why not simply deliver the Hebrews at once, without challenge or opposition? What is his purpose for multiplying and prolonging the plagues?

THE PURPOSE IN THE PLAGUE

"Don't wanna wide de twike!" John was adamant, stamping his foot with all the imperiousness a two-year-old could muster. I sighed. I had been trying for weeks to teach him to pedal, all to no avail.

"Fine," I sat wearily on the bench. "Go play, then, but don't just leave your tricycle out like that. You need to take care of it. People steal stuff in this neighbourhood." Oblivious, John raced off to fling himself on the swings. Then I noticed Jeffy, a boy from our apartment complex, eyeing the abandoned trike. Built like a barn, and with a fiery temper, little Jeffy was a year older than John and used to getting his way. The two boys had never exactly hit it off as friends, possibly due to the fact that John couldn't quite pronounce his name correctly and tended to refer to him as "Fuffy." A misnomer if ever there was one.

Glancing covertly (he was, I swear, a cunning child), Fuffy slowly headed for the prize. Oh, oh, I thought, here it comes. Somehow, John must have noticed his playmate's suspicious stalking gait; he promptly jumped off the swing and ran to the tricycle just as Fuffy reached out to grasp the handlebars. Both toddlers stared hard at each other, but John's grip was half-hearted and Fuffy was one buff kid.

"Leggo!" Fuffy snarled, menacingly. Narrowing his eyes, he yanked at the bike.

"No." John tightened his grip an instant before the powerhouse pull, and stood his ground. Attaboy, I thought, surprised and impressed by my son's resistance.

"Gimmee!" Furious, Fuffy began to scream and yell, threatening to pummel my son with his fist, all the while pulling on the bike with his other hand.

John was clearly taken aback by the vehemence of the attack. Fuffy had several inches and at least twenty pounds over my son. This boy was going to take him down. When John glanced uncertainly in my direction, I spoke out with all the confidence I could muster.

"You," I called out loudly, "are a Big Boy. And that," I said, pointing, "is Your Bike."

John heard the conviction in my voice, and somehow believed my words. "My bike," he said, tightening his grip. "Go away."

The more that Barnyard Boy screamed and threatened, the more stubborn John grew. The bike was his. Okay, he had never actually wanted it before but, darn it, it was his. And now that someone else clearly wanted to take it away from him, my son decided that it must be worth fighting for. And he was a Big Boy and could stand up to this bully; Mom said so.

In the end, bruised but determined, John kept his bike. As Fuffy was swept up by his embarrassed mother, John astounded me by promptly mounting his tricycle and pedalling back to the swings.

"My twicycle," He muttered audibly. "Bad Fuffy."

***

I've heard it said that, politically, we do not truly *own* what we haven't fought for. When we are challenged, we are forced to decide whether the fight is actually worth it. Do we care enough to meet opposition squarely, to stand our ground and defend what we believe in? In these instances, God is not indifferent, but alert to see what we'll do. In the conflict over the tricycle, I considered intervening, but I decided to watch and see what would happen after determination lit my son's eyes. I allowed the confrontation, just as God allowed Pharaoh to oppose Moses. (Besides, Jeffy scared me.) Not only did Moses face the wrath of Pharaoh, but the betrayal of his own people challenged his tenuous grasp of his identity as a leader. God allowed these challenges, and, in the Book of Exodus, there is a purpose in each plague.

With each trial, it's as if God were asking, "How much do you Hebrews really desire your freedom? How much does it matter, and what cost are you willing to pay?" These slaves are having their appetite sharpened, because, in the end, they will be unstoppable in the ferocity of their rebellion. They will own their freedom in a way that only those who have had to fight for it could possibly understand, just as Moses owns his identity as a leader, as each challenge forces him to return to God, reassess his direction, lean in to conflict, and reassert his calling. As the plagues continue, each victory not only increases the glory attributed to God, but also the credibility of his servant Moses.

The Hebrews do not fail to note Moses's refusal to be derailed; they see his dignity in the face of Pharaoh's tantrums and petty megalomania. They also see Moses refusing to take their own complaints personally, but instead consistently taking the issues to their God. By deferring in this way, Moses demonstrates that he is not just their leader, but one of them, speaking to God on their behalf about their concerns. This behaviour as a leader in the face of trial and failure builds a sense of "team" that will be vital to their future survival as a new culture in a hostile land. Team-building is, in fact, one of the most significant factors in establishing effective leadership that will survive crisis. Lasting solutions can only be achieved and maintained when "the people with the problem" go through a process together, to become "the people with the solution."

The plagues also served as an opportunity for God, through Moses, to re-cast vision and strengthen the corporate identity of the Hebrews. God was proving himself superior to various Egyptian deities and claiming the Hebrews as his special people. The plagues of blood, frogs, gnats, flies, boils, hail, locusts, and darkness only fell upon their enemies. The death of the first-born sons did not touch the Hebrews. They were God's people; with each victory, and Pharaoh's subsequently maddening refusals to release them, their desire for freedom only grew more intense. Facing opposition compels us to clarify what we really want. Just as John needed Jeffy's tantrum to recognize that he really did want to keep his bike, so opposition reinforces both vision and identity.

It's a complex procedure, with the constant threat that we may be derailed by the repeated challenges. We may tire easily, much as muscles being strengthened through resistance training. We must keep the goal in sight and focus our attention on what God has said to us. "You're a big boy," I told little John, "and that is your bike." God allows and even initiates conflict so that we might battle to take ownership of the identity he has pronounced over us and the vision he has cast for us. Understanding this key concept does much to help us avoid despair when trials and disappointments come our way. Knowing that "...*in all things God works for the good of those who love him, who have been called according to his purpose*" (Romans 8:28), we can be confident in each crisis, even thankful that God is—through this trial—demonstrating his confidence in us. Both James and Romans reassure us that suffering (the words used refer specifically to opposition and persecution) are to be welcomed as opportunities for growth and change. James 1:2–4 tells us:

> *Consider it pure joy, my brothers and sisters, whenever you face trials of many kinds, because you know that the testing of your faith produces perseverance. Let perseverance finish its work so that you may be mature and complete, not lacking anything.*

And Romans 5:3–5 assures us that "...*suffering produces perseverance; perseverance, character; and character, hope. And hope does not put us to shame, because God's love has been poured out into our hearts through the Holy Spirit, who has been given to us.*"

Through nine arduous plagues, Moses re-casts this vision to the suffering Hebrews. They need to persevere; they need to hang on. God's credibility, and that of his servant Moses, is tested and proven again and again. Then, when the Hebrews are oh-so-ready to book it out of Egypt, God announces the final plague. And the people, ready to run, are instead told to pause.

A SACRED PAUSE

Moses is told that the last plague will be the definitive event that results in freedom for the people. Here, as elsewhere in Exodus, ritualistic action is used to celebrate theophany, as God instructs the Hebrews to prepare themselves for the tenth, and last, plague. The rich symbolism of the Passover imparts to Moses and to his people an identity that cannot be shaken, a certainty of who they are in God's sight. The annual, ritual remembrance guards them against the self-absorption of fear, the seduction of idolatry, and the apathy of prosperity that will one day threaten them in the Promised Land. This institution, as with that of the Feast of Unleavened Bread and the Dedication of the First-Born (Exodus 13), is a tangible, commemorative event, an opportunity for both solemn remembrance and sober preparation, much like the sacrament of the Lord's Supper is for Christians today. For the Israelites, the Passover was to be a "*lasting ordinance*" (Exodus 12:14) that would embrace past, present, and future in a single moment, a kind of sacred pause.

For the Jewish people, the escape from Egypt is the crucial event of universal history. It is also the source of all biblical language regarding salvation and liberation, including the salvation of the cross. When God instructs the Israelites to commemorate all that he has said and done for them, he is in essence instructing them to remember who he *is*. This is not a command to hold a eulogy; it is a command to hold a celebration of a very personal nature, directing thoughts and thanksgiving toward the one who has delivered and established his people.

These celebrations act as a stabilizing force to unite the Israelites in their corporate identity, national existence, and properly-aligned relationship with God. In Deuteronomy 8:19, God tells the Israelites, "*If you ever forget the Lord your God and follow other gods and worship and bow down to them, I testify against you today that you will surely be destroyed.*" In Exodus 13, the rules concerning these rituals are entrusted to the fathers to be faithfully passed down to their children (13:8, 14), presumably the first-born sons in particular. Although it seems that Passover, the Feast of Unleavened Bread, and the sacrifice accompanying the redemption of the first-born were not observed with any regularity in the wilderness (the specific manner of this service was to begin once they entered the Promised Land, see Exodus 13:5, 11), with each new child came an opportunity to repeat the story, review the instructions, and renew their anticipatory focus on the fulfillment of God's promises.

The opening two verses of Chapter 13 have Yahweh declare his ownership of all first-born males of Israel, whether animal or human. They are to be set apart. This commandment is a powerful counterpart to the plague that claimed the lives of Egypt's first-born sons already, a stark reminder that this sacrifice belonged to Yahweh and could be enforced regardless of religious loyalties. Exodus 13:14–15 says:

> ... *"With a mighty hand the Lord brought us out of Egypt, out of the land of slavery. When Pharaoh stubbornly refused to let us go, the Lord killed the firstborn of both people and animals in Egypt. This is why I sacrifice to the Lord the first male offspring of every womb and redeem each of my firstborn sons."*

By dedicating and redeeming each first-born male child, the Hebrews show that they are claiming their identity as God's people. Not only does every first-born male belong to God, the nation of Israel as a whole is also referred to as God's first-born son (Exodus 4:22).

In this context, Jesus's death illustrates this sacrificial principle. Destined to be the one, perfect redeeming sacrifice for humanity, Jesus was also the first-born son of God. Jesus fulfilled the intended role of Israel as God's faithful first-born son, perfect in life, sacrificial death, and resurrection.

The blood of the Passover lamb becomes a symbol for life, that which must be spilled in order for redemption to take place. The unleavened *"bread of affliction"* (as it is called in Deuteronomy 16:3) becomes a symbol of divine deliverance; as Israel recalls their hasty departure from captivity in Egypt, this bread will be hereafter eaten in solemn but celebratory remembrance. Both the blood and the bread have their symbolism fulfilled in Christ, as he instigates the sacrament of communion. In the years to come, Israel would annually rehearse their past, trust for the present, and be assured of their future, through observing these rituals. In this same way, Jesus directs our eyes back to the cross with every celebration of the sacrament of the Last Supper, comforting us in the present and assuring us of our eternal future. As with Yahweh and Israel, Jesus calls his followers to a sacred pause of remembrance.

With Christ's first disciples, this pause was perhaps confusing, even ominous, as he broke the bread and passed the cup. They, like the Israelites of Exodus, could not anticipate the trials to come. But God, in disciplining his people through rituals that force us to pause and reflect, ensures that we not despair when faced with trials. We are to remember God's promises, as if they are written on our foreheads (Exodus 13:9, 16). Israel would face a terrifying escape across a miraculously parted sea, followed by forty years of following a pillar of cloud and fire, camping in waterless wastelands, and facing war, pestilence, culinary tedium, and terrifying theophany. In the future, Christ's disciples would see their rabbi nailed to a tree, and then they would face the unimaginable horrors of persecution. Christians today are weighed down by millennia spent waiting for Christ to return, tempted to languish and give in to apathy or worldliness. To remember is for us, as it was for the Hebrews in Egypt, a matter of life and death.

With blood on the doorpost to ward off the Angel of Death, the Hebrews are instructed to pause and remember; in doing so, they will save their very lives. When Jesus broke the bread and passed the cup of the New Covenant at the celebration of Passover he said, "...*do this in remembrance of me*" (Luke 22:19). At these words, the disciples would have remembered the instructions given by Moses. As with the Israelites, they were about to face trials that would test their faith beyond imagining. To forget the words of Jesus would be disastrous, as they faced his crucifixion and the persecution ahead. But, as with the disciples, each time we observe the covenant we remember *whose* we are: a purchased people.

That lesson is driven home that fateful night in Egypt when, during the last plague, the sounds of anguish fill the air. Death comes to Egypt, to cattle and pauper and Pharaoh alike, as every first-born male dies at the hand of God. The Angel of Death, seeing the blood on the lintels, passes over the Hebrews and they escape unscathed. By the time the Hebrews finally leave, they are practically given the red carpet out of Egypt, with their oppressors loading them with gold and silver and other valuables. Moses then mobilizes six hundred thousand men (plus or including women and children, for a total that is unclear but nonetheless staggering) and leads them out of Egypt.

Triumphant and united, they depart for parts unknown, praising their God and confident in their leader. The panic at the Red Sea gives way to incredulity and shouts of joy as even the waves get out of their way. Nothing can stop them, freedom is theirs! Moses, in reflecting, might have even given thanks that God had not allowed it to be too easy a win. Even though he faced opposition and the criticism of his own people, the challenges they overcame together surely served to increase their solidarity.

Until they got tired. Until they got thirsty. Until they were bored stupid with manna.

WHO NEEDS THIS!

Sliding my guitar pick between the strings, I smiled. It had been a particularly well-received set. The congregation was really into these high-energy renewal songs now and entered in enthusiastically right from the first riff. As I left the stage, I saw my father-in-law approaching. A prophetic word? I hoped so. Certainly, some commendation, at the very least. My father-in-law, Dr. John White, was a retired psychiatrist, and a well-known author and speaker at that time. His opinion mattered very much to me.

We walked together to the back of the church, and there, Dad fixed me with his piercing blue eyes. Oh, oh.

"Do you think," he asked, "that you are under an anointing?"

I hesitated. What did he even mean? What would anointing feel like? I wasn't shaking or roaring. But other people were, while worship was going on. I replied that I certainly felt that I was under a divine hand of favour, but did not know if that was the same as anointing.

Dad nodded. "Anointing," he explained patiently, "is something that God gives you for the sake of those you have been sent to serve." My happy bubble of self-centredness popped abruptly.

"What is that supposed to mean?" I asked defensively. Somehow, I knew that I was not going to appreciate his answer.

"I think," my father-in-law said pointedly, "that you are not serving them. I think that you are manipulating them. That is a kind of witchcraft, you know."

"What the heck!" I was hurt and furious. Who needs this? Deep down, I suspected that he was right, but found myself angrily

reactive. "It's what they want! They want to be manipulated, Dad! I'm just giving them what they want!"

Dad shook his head. "There is no 'they,' darling. It's all just 'us.'"

***

I had always been, as so many musicians are, addicted to praise. A "good set" was one in which the audience responded with enthusiastic clapping or tears. I had always been aware of the danger of giving in to the temptation to "play to the crowd," and often struggled to keep myself focused on the Lord and not on dour faces, bored yawns, or—as in the case of my youngest child—distracted nose-picking in the front row. It was impossible to maintain a straight course, impossible to completely avoid the opposite extremes of either self-doubt or power-tripping. But, if I couldn't walk the fine line, I thought, I could at least keep my zigzags as tight as possible. Doing that pleased no one, of course; neither stylistically nor musically. There must be some way to engage the majority, I fretted. Then the Renewal hit.

Tagged the "Toronto Blessing" in the 1990s, a wave of Holy Spirit-infused phenomena swept across North America, Europe, and beyond. Classic manifestations of the charismatic were rampant, as well as more unusual behaviours, such as roaring like "the Lion of Judah," chanting key words or phrases in—or until reaching—an ecstatic state, and dramatic physical jerking and shaking. I don't doubt that many who experienced this renewal were deeply touched and refreshed in their love and commitment to Jesus. People came hungry, expectant, and ready to meet God. There was faith in each service, including in our own small church, and worship took off. It was to be the making—and the breaking—of many, including myself.

At first, I welcomed the change as more people enthusiastically threw themselves into worship. Closed eyes, hands in the air, and bodies swaying was enough to convince any musician that what they were doing was working. Our pastor at that time coached the worship team before each service, encouraging—even insisting—that we keep excitement levels high by playing certain songs. I complied, as did the other worship leaders because, as I said, it was "working." But Dad was right, of course. I had, in the rush of renewal fervour, allowed myself to use both God and others to satisfy my own ambitious desires. I ceased to identify with the people to whom I had been sent, ceased wanting to serve them. Instead, I was asking *them* to serve *me*. "We" somehow became "me" and "them." I was not under any anointing. I was simply doing whatever I had to do in order to get and keep their approval. Because it *worked*.

With wide-spread renewalism in our church creating a kind of musical and stylistic homogeneity in worship, I was finally able to please everyone—and my father-in-law was calling me a witch. Not a high point in any musical career! What could I do? Wise man that he was, Dad offered no opinions, but told me to pray about it. I didn't want to, but I did anyway. And that night I had a dream.

ME, THEM, US?

In my dream, I saw a North American map with three rivers flowing across from the east coast to the west coast. They were, I saw, rivers of renewal and of the Holy Spirit. I felt excited until I heard a voice, saying, "Let my rivers flow across the land; bring my blessing, bring my vengeance." I woke suddenly, upset and confused. How could a blessing also be a judgment?

Later, much too late in the case of our own church, I saw how this attitude of "us" and "them" could bring about the downfall of many a pastor, church leader, and congregation. This was not to say that the Toronto Blessing was of the Devil; quite the contrary, I believe many who received this fresh manifestation of God lived richer, fuller, and more sacrificial lives. But others also fell into a self-serving idolatry of the experiential, causing them to disdain non-charismatics and dangerously isolate themselves as individuals or as congregations, therefore falling into grievous sin. For some, that sin was pride, the arrogant criticism of the mainstream Body of Christ. For others, it was sexual sin. One pastor went on to have numerous extra-marital affairs over the course of at least seven years before his sin was exposed.

The same experience that brought blessing for some brought divine vengeance on others. The individualism that is so much a part of Western culture became our downfall. The only safety seemed to be in strict accountability, a community that dared to speak truth in love to one another. But, in the grip of subjectivity, where manifestations were equated with godliness and spiritual superiority, very few dared to speak any warnings, for fear of being told they were "quenching the Spirit." Dad was right: there was no place for a "me" and "them" attitude in the church. It needed to be "us," or we would be destroyed when God's blessing came with his wrath.

Convicted by my father-in-law's assessment of my worship leading, I vowed to do things differently. I spent more time in prayer, seeking to hear from God regarding which songs to use each Sunday. I tried to follow the lead of the Holy Spirit, but stopped catering to the charismatic. To my dismay, I became convinced that I should move away from using songs that focused heavily on individualistic experiences. This limited my song selection radically, as the bulk of songs written during that time were highly subjective. The vast number of popular songs had lyrics that focused on expressing, usually in first person singular, our "feelings" and our "needs." Lyrics such as, "I'm desperate for you," "I need your presence," and "Let your power come" were the worship vocabulary of the day. Cutting back on these songs left me in a panic. What on Earth would I sing?

I searched the old hymnals and found songs that spoke of corporate praise and thanksgiving, and spoke truth about who God was; these songs were, now, immensely meaningful to me. Here were songs that anyone could sing, at any time, in any emotional state. These songs allowed us to express true things about God, regardless of how we felt. I was convinced that, like the Psalmist, we needed to *Ascribe to the Lord the glory due his name...*" (Psalm 29:2). However, the majority of these hymns also spoke of God in the third person (i.e.: "he, him"), and I maintained the conviction that the intimacy brought through the renewal was genuine and of paramount importance. There began difficult months of putting together worship sets with songs that expressed true things *about* God, *to* God. (i.e.: "God, *you are* holy"). Sifting through the new songs, I discarded the peppier ones in favour of those that had more simple and straightforward tunes. I resurrected older hymns. I was positive that I was doing the right thing. I was obeying God. Surely, he would reward me. Surely now I would have my anointing. The result? I bombed.

The congregation stared, that awful deer-in-the-headlights look that every musician dreads. My new approach was definitely not what they wanted. The pastor repeatedly took me aside and asked me to pick different songs. It was back to "me" and "them" again. I shook my head helplessly, and, in the end, was slowly weaned off the worship schedule. It was humiliating, and I was angry with God. But I knew I couldn't go back. I would go home and rail at the heavens, and yell at my father-in-law. Why me? The other worship leaders were flying high, enjoying the renewalist fervour. Why wasn't God convicting *them*? Why did they get to have all the fun? I felt like God's least favoured child and resented it deeply. But I had no choice; perhaps for other leaders, worship wasn't manipulating or self-serving. But, for me, it had become a clearly exposed sin. I was plagued with self-doubt; perhaps I wasn't meant to be a leader at all. All I knew was that I couldn't cross the line that God had drawn in the sand. So, I put my guitar away and sulked.

The renewal carried on without me, of course. I still believed, as I do now, that this was an authentic move by God. I still supported those who sought a close, experiential relationship with him, and continued to pray for this for myself and others. But now I understood that the anointing I sought couldn't be just for "me" alone, it need to be for "us." But, even as I grew in my understanding for the need for a corporate identity in the renewal, I noticed that some renewalists seemed to be intentionally creating an aura of spiritual exclusivity through music, church vernacular, even hair and clothing styles, and approaches to prayer ministry. Far from making the renewal accessible to others, this actually limited its effectiveness. Some leaders in the movement were known to make jokes about conservative, mainstream, or cautiously non-charismatic Christians. "Let your Spirit fall on them," I heard one say mockingly from the stage, "whether they want it or not!"

Such subtle ridicule only widened the rift between "me" and "them." Songs continued to be largely hyperbolic and emotionally subjective, leaving those who didn't feel desperate, impassioned, or ravished in their soul to stand in awkward silence, or else sing in clumsy pretense. We were leaving them out; it was wrong. More, it was unnecessary. Yet, even as I yearned to see a more inclusive approach, I envied those who belonged to the enchanted inner circle. I was back on the playground, banned from the sandbox. I wanted in, yet was loath to embrace fully what was being modelled. Could I be one of them and still be me? Apparently not, I thought, remembering the criticism about my song choices. I had done everything that I thought God was asking of me, and it didn't work. We were not "us," we were "me" and "them." I had lost the solidarity that I needed to be a leader. It was hugely frustrating.

My frustration was minor, obviously, compared to that of Moses.

GRAVES OF CRAVINGS

"I have a face, you know," my daughter Robin commented, half-jokingly. The infant in her arms paid no attention, wriggling furiously in his attempt to find and latch on to the sole object of his affections.

Sighing, the new mom resignedly began to unbutton her blouse. "I try singing. Cuddling. Even blowing in his face," she muttered with a wry smile. "but does he even make eye contact? Heck, no."

Her husband Jason chuckled. At the sound of his voice, baby Judah instantly swung his face towards him, and smiled. Mama was not impressed.

"Really?" she demanded. "That's all it takes? Daddy just has to walk in the room and make a noise?"

Turning back to the source of all maternal comfort, Judah began to nurse hungrily, eyes closing in contentment. His mom sighed again.

"Yup, that's me," she shook her head, smiling. "A boob with a face attached."

***

God drafted Moses to do a job that involved being a priest, a prophet, and a military strategist; all the Hebrews seemed to care about was whether or not he would provide food and drink for their stomachs. Like my daughter, I imagine he felt like nothing more than a meal service at times. The Hebrews' approval of his leadership seemed to last precisely as long as it took to burn the calories of their last dinner. Throughout the wilderness exile, Moses is challenged time and again by the criticism of the people he seeks to lead. Whether from fear (Exodus 14:11), thirst (Exodus 15:22–25; 17:3), hunger (Exodus 16:2–3), ambition (Numbers 16:11, 41; 17:5, 10), boredom ("Manna *again?*" Numbers 11:1–6), or pure idolatrous lust (Exodus 32:1), the people of Israel continue to resent Moses, and at times reject him outright. Regardless of how dramatic, how frequent, or how recent the miraculous signs and wonders might be, hunger and thirst continue to determine their perception of him:

> *In the desert the whole community grumbled against Moses and Aaron. The Israelites said to them, "If only we had died by the Lord's hand in Egypt! There we sat around pots of meat and ate all the food we wanted, but you have brought us out into this desert to starve this entire assembly to death."* (Exodus 16:2–3)

Was it wrong for the Israelites to crave meat in the time of manna? They could hardly pretend that their appetites were satisfied—God sees, and knows, our mortal frame and its weakness. But rather than come to him in humble supplication for a change in the menu, their craving led them to complain bitterly, flinging harsh accusations against God and his appointed representative, Moses. It doesn't seem like the people did anything to restrain their cravings or curb their appetites. Instead, they nurtured their discontent by yielding to and indulging in complaint and slander. The Lord's judgment upon them was a slaughter so extensive that the place where they camped became known as *Kibroth Hattaavah*, "Graves of Craving," "*because there they buried the people who had craved other food*" (Numbers 11:34). God and Moses were, to them, simply a means to an end, a way of having their immediate desires satisfied. Sound familiar? Certainly, new mothers, like my daughter, can relate to the frustration of being seen merely as a source of food, when really the food itself is a sign of a much greater gift of unconditional, sacrificial love.

Far from respecting Moses as their Deliverer, the Israelites looked upon him as more of a "delivery man." Generations later, Jesus, the Bread of Heaven and Fount of Living Waters, was also hounded by hungry crowds:

> *Jesus said to them, "Very truly I tell you, it is not Moses who has given you the bread from heaven, but it is my Father who gives you the true bread from heaven. For the bread of God is the bread that comes down from heaven and gives life to the world." "Sir," they said, "always give us this bread." Then Jesus declared, "I am the bread of life. Whoever comes to me will never go hungry, and whoever believes in me will never be thirsty. But as I told you, you have seen me and still you do not believe."* (John 6:32–36)

Cravings are natural, often a reflection of a healthy appetite for those things our bodies actually need, things that are meant to sustain us. Irritating as it may have been, our daughter knew that she couldn't take offence that her newborn only had eyes for his source of milk. Babies crave milk. The dehydrated jogger craves water, the injured in shock crave sugar. God designed us so that we often instinctively crave what we need. Yet cravings are not always good, as the Hebrews learned at the Graves of Craving, *Kibroth Hattaavah*. Giving in to the cravings of an angry, complaining heart can be deadly. There is a vast difference between craving what one needs and demanding what one wants.

Several years ago, the leadership team for our church's woman's ministry was involved in a process of mission clarification. We felt that we needed to redefine our goals and priorities for our Wednesday morning women's event. Throwing the discussion wide open, we were astounded at the vastly divergent perspectives regarding the mission of this program.

In our desire to be culturally relevant, we designed the morning around a weekly feature that would focus on the interests of the women in the community. This ranged anywhere from garden clubs to social activism. Our attempt to keep the ambience appealing led to the development of a decor committee, and our value of relationship motivated us to appoint and train hostesses and greeters. To appreciate this generation's hunger for self-improvement, busy schedule, and attention span that was being shortened daily by their exposure to social media, we designed a dozen or so classes to be held simultaneously each trimester and actively solicited teachers. Conscious of our demographic, we arranged for daycare with state-of-the-art security monitors and pagers. A group of polished female musicians worked to bring high quality music, searching intently for acceptable secular songs with messages that would align with that week's feature. Women were coming to Christ, bringing their spouses to Alpha and their children to church clubs. As a program that intentionally focused on being an entry-level ministry for non-Christians we—well—kicked butt.

But, as time went by and we sought to move the women more purposefully toward a deeper engagement with the gospel, we hit a wall. Attendees began to complain. They wanted more time to sit around their tables, eat snacks we provided for them, and visit with their friends while their children were cared for by volunteers. Our lofty vision for reaching the lost was in danger of becoming a cheap babysitting service. By catering to their cravings, we had created an insatiable sense of entitlement. How could we meet real needs without giving in to selfish, harmful cravings? There were other demands, more complaints. It was difficult to remember what our real mandate was, as women complained about song choices, the dearth of gluten-free appies, and their allergies to scented candles. It took grit to stay the course and not allow ourselves to become distracted by their expectations, which only grew as the program became more and more successful.

To stay focused as a leadership team, we often needed to meet together and re-cast the vision, reminding ourselves why we were there and who we really were. Without a clear and confident grasp of our identity and calling in being *sent* to the unreached, we had no hope of resisting the defining opinions of others. Losing sight of our mandate left us vulnerable to being swayed by the masses, directed by the most strident voice, and held hostage to hidden agendas. Reggie McNeal points out the urgency of having our identity and calling clearly defined and in focus at all times: "Not coming to a clear understanding of what you have been called to do leaves you vulnerable to completing agendas and imposing personalities in your ministry world."[26] If we weren't careful, their desires would define us, their cravings become our graves. How can we respond to such an attack?

First and foremost, we recognized that God was allowing the criticism and complaining. If we responded with faith and focus, the challenge would serve to strengthen of our resolve and clarify our sense of calling. This is true of any attack from criticism and complaint. Early on in the Exodus story, we see that Moses meets these crises by deflecting the criticism and complaint to the one to whom it is, in fact, ultimately directed.

Moses continually refused to be distracted into a posture of self-defence, but instead defers to the source of his authority, the author of his identity. "*Who are we?*" he exclaims in response to their complaints. "*You are not grumbling against us, but against the Lord*" (Exodus 16:8). As mentioned earlier, his skilful management of the attack not only built credibility, but allowed him to frequently re-cast his vision. By stepping back from our own natural tendency to take criticism personally, we can draw the attention away from our person and back to the issues. Faced with an angry, thirsty mob, Moses "*cried out to the Lord*" (Exodus 15:25). God not only vindicated and upheld the authority of his servant, but used the opportunity to remind the people about the ground rules:

> *If you listen carefully to the Lord your God and do what is right in his eyes, if you pay attention to his commands and keep all his decrees, I will not bring on you any of the diseases I brought on the Egyptians, for I am the Lord, who heals you.* (Exodus 15:26)

"Remember the plagues?" God seems to be saying, "Do you really want to get on my bad side?"

As the leadership team, we decided to take the challenges and criticism and turn them into opportunities to re-cast vision and to reinforce identity. We took a stand. Our program existed to reach the lost, and that would dictate every priority. Our sent-ness defined us. Those

---

[26] McNeal, *A Work of Heart,* 106.

who were either looking for a Bible study or hoping for free daycare were welcome to go elsewhere. The result? Church-goers ceased their grumbling and caught the vision; volunteer involvement multiplied. Those women who rolled their eyes at the "church-y" aspects of our program grew to respect and even admire us when we unapologetically reminded them that they were, after all, in a church. Attendance soared, and we hired a part-time staff person to direct the growth. As a leadership team, we became even more committed to each other and to the vision.

If we are not convinced of who God has called us to be, and to whom he has sent us, we will be hard pressed to defend ourselves before those who criticize us, much less before an enemy who plots our destruction. If he can weaken our identity, and cause us to doubt who we are and to whom we have been sent, he wins. Sometimes the challenges are gruelling and go on for years, requiring that we, like Moses, have patience and endurance that only God can supply. At other times, the attacks are vicious and brief, making it even more imperative that we not be caught off-guard.

"IF YOU ARE..."

Where Moses endured forty years in the desert with grumbling malcontents, Jesus endured an intense forty days of direct Satanic opposition and temptation. These temptations were designed to not only to provoke sinful action, but to sow seeds of self-doubt in the divinely-affirmed identity of the Son of God.

In Matthew 4:1–11, Satan attempts to goad Jesus into proving who he is with this repeated refrain: "*If you are the son of God...*" The Devil tries to get Jesus to turn stone into bread, to throw himself off the temple, and to bow down to him in exchange for all the kingdoms of the world.

Yet Jesus refuses to be baited. He knows he doesn't have to prove anything. Instead, Jesus deflects and defers back to his Father, quoting from scripture:

> "*It is written: 'Man shall not live on bread alone, but on every word that comes from the mouth of God.'*"... "*It is also written: 'Do not*

put the Lord your God to the test.'"... "For it is written: 'Worship the Lord your God, and serve him only.'" (Matthew 4:4, 6, 10)

Jesus resists the Devil by citing these three texts from Deuteronomy 8:3; 6:16; 6:13, all of which refer to trials the people of Israel faced in the wilderness (the manna, testing God at Massah, and worshipping the golden calf). The Israelites failed these trials, but Jesus doesn't because he refuses to be distracted from his mission. By dismissing Satan, Jesus receives validation of his identity, as angels come and minister to him (4:11).

The attacks on our identity are real and painful. We will be tempted to abandon our mission and turn our backs on those to whom we have been sent. These challenges will come when we are weakest: tired, hungry, lonely, grumpy, ashamed, sick, and wounded. Jesus faced temptations after forty days of fast, and the Israelites during their forty years in the desert. In the desert, Moses falls prey to the temptation to strike a rock in anger and self-aggrandizing pride, miraculously providing water; Jesus is challenged by Satan to provide food for himself, but he resists. Poised precariously on the pinnacle of the temple, Satan dares Jesus to call upon the angels to rescue him from a fall. "Feed yourself! Save yourself! Prove yourself!" Satan lashes out. "Who do you think you are?"

Later, hanging on a cursed cross, bearing the weight of sin so heinous that it demanded that God himself turn his back on his own son, Jesus faces the desolation of utter abandonment. Forsaken, Jesus cries out in a loud voice, *"'Eli, Eli, lema sabachthani?' (which means 'My God, my God, why have you forsaken me?')"* (Matthew 27:46). The Hebrews in the desert—faced with the absence of their leader Moses for the forty days he met with God on Mt. Sinai—flounder. Where was their leader? Why had he forsaken them? What if he never came back? What if this God of theirs was not real after all? Their identities waver, their hopes fade, and they worship an idol of their own making. Jesus, in contrast, clings to his identity until death tears away the veil, and he once again sees his Father face-to-face.

Jesus refused to take his identity in anything other than the one who had defined him, named him, and sent him. His mission involved identifying himself with the people to whom he had been sent. This demanded he face all challenges as a man, wholly human in his resources. Christ's human-ness endured demonic accusations and the vitriolic criticisms of his fellow man. Even when his heart broke at Judas's betrayal. Even when he wept for the very city that condemned him to death. Even when he was spat upon, laughed at, and scorned as he hung upon a cross:

> …*"You who are going to destroy the temple and build it in three days, save yourself! Come down from the cross, if you are the Son of God!" In the same way the chief priests, the teachers of the law and the elders mocked him. "He saved others," they said, "but he can't save himself! He's the king of Israel! Let him come down now from the cross, and we will believe in him."* (Matthew 27:40–42)

"If you are…" This last challenge was, perhaps, the hardest of all to endure, as those most in need of saving arrogantly disdained Christ's sacrifice. If only Jesus would rip his hands and feet from the nails in a display of power, then they would believe in him. "Give us what we crave!" they cry, "And then we will follow you!" Instead, Jesus gives up his life, knowing that this is the only way he can truly fulfill his mission: "*'Now my soul is troubled, and what shall I say? 'Father, save me from this hour'? No, it was for this very reason I came to this hour'*" (John 12:27).

The goal is death to Self, remember. The prize? Unspeakable intimacy.

ME, US, HIM

I stared up at the underside of a chair. I had no idea how I had managed to roll underneath, and the sight of shoes and Bibles and stockinged feet set me off laughing again. What on Earth was happening?

"Oi!" my friend from New Zealand peered down at me in bemusement. "What are you doing under there? What's goin' on?"

I sputtered in an attempt to answer coherently, but it was hopeless. All around me I could hear the waves of hilarity rising and falling like the surf of a southern sea, as three thousand people were buffeted by what was termed "holy laughter."

It was the height of the Renewal of the 1990s, the so-called "Toronto Blessing," and I had arrived that evening at a large church event meant to fan the flames of worship and moving in the Spirit. I came feeling cynical, skeptical, and depressed. I had been wrestling with resentment over the excesses at our church, not so much on theological grounds as from the sense that I was, yet again, a misfit: too restrained for Charismatics, too subjective and emotional for Conservatives. The sense of not belonging anywhere had been wearing me down. And then—wham!

When the laughter finally subsided, I found myself weeping, a not-unheard-of phenomena following a catharsis of this kind. Suddenly, I felt myself being pulled out from under the chair and lifted, with gentle but strong hands under my armpits. I was helpless, limp, and disoriented.

"It's okay," one of the young men said. *What's okay? I wondered, confused.* "He'll give you the words. It will be all right." *What will be all right? Why weren't my legs working?*

My next memory was of being carried up to the stage, propped up in front of a microphone and being told to sing. *Sing what? How?* My weeping had not yet abated, yet I felt intense yearning instead of sadness.

"Sing the song of the Bride," the conference speaker said, fixing me with a piercing look. "Sing the song of the Church, calling out to her Beloved."

I had no idea what this meant, but as a pianist played a series of perfect fifths, I remembered the words from Ezekiel 16:1–8:

> "On the day you were born your cord was not cut, nor were you washed with water to make you clean, nor were you rubbed with salt or wrapped in cloths. No one looked on you with pity or had compassion enough to do any of these things for you. Rather, you were thrown out into the open field, for on the day you were born you were

despised. Then I passed by and saw you kicking about in your blood, and as you lay there in your blood I said to you, 'Live!' I made you grow like a plant of the field. You grew and developed and entered puberty. Your breasts had formed and your hair had grown, yet you were stark naked. Later I passed by, and when I looked at you and saw that you were old enough for love, I spread the corner of my garment over you and covered your naked body. I gave you my solemn oath and entered into a covenant with you, declares the Sovereign Lord, and you became mine."

"We come," the words poured out of my mouth before I even realized that I was singing. "We wait for you, alone and cast out, covered in our own blood…" I wept as I thanked the Lord for seeking and rescuing the outcast: those who, like me, felt they had been driven into the desert, abandoned and filthy, wallowing in loneliness and self-pity. I felt as though I were singing not with my own voice, but with a million other voices. I was not "me" but "us," singing the song of the corporate Bride of Christ, the Church universal.

The pianist sang a response, taking the part of the Bridegroom. "Live!" he commanded. "I claim you, I call you by name. I cover you, I clean you and anoint you; you are Mine."

The response in the room was electric. Some shrieked and fell down in seizures, later to testify of demonic deliverance. Others wailed, as if suddenly aware of their uncleanness and desperate need for cleansing. It was chaos, and prayer ministry teams sought to deal with the agitated crowd. Then slowly it faded, and the band picked up and led us back into worship and a sweet sense of God's presence prevailed.

My escorts helped me descend the stage as, with shaking limbs, I sat down again next to my Kiwi companion. Chairs were scattered across the auditorium, some still lying on their sides, where their occupants had tumbled out of them. I smiled weakly at my friend's incredulous stare.

"Oi," he said again, shaking his head.
Oi, indeed.

***

Many were touched that night, and I was profoundly changed. "Me" had become, for a brief moment, "us." I wanted more. Yet I was also cautious; I had seen too many people "slain in the Spirit" only to go on to become self-absorbed conference junkies, going from church to church in search of the ecstatic, hooked on the anointing of the Spirit in the way that an addict is ever looking for the next "fix." I likened it to becoming obsessed with the physical act of sex, choosing to forget that the role of sex should be to enhance intimacy for the sake of the relationship, not merely for a brief moment of narcissistic pleasure. I was "renewed," but I wasn't ready to identify with renewalists. But after what had just happened to me, I assumed that God was clearly sending me to that side of the playground. Excited, I found myself hoping that this was my chance, finally, to be on the inside, to leave the fringe for the coveted Inner Circle.

My father-in-law was again instrumental in my life during this time. As an author, international speaker, and retired psychiatrist, his perspectives were invaluable. As a man of God, he had great wisdom. And as a dad, he cut to the quick. Coming to speak with me shortly after my experience, Dad asked me what was different now in my life. I replied that I felt as if God were closer, more real, and infinitely more precious to me.

"What should I do?" I asked him. I imagined myself being sent to support some itinerant Charismatic ministry, learning to move powerfully in the gifts of the Spirit, blessing multitudes, speaking at conferences. Typical post-anointing ego-tripping, I suppose.

Dad responded. "Well, darling, I should begin a disciplined habit of daily devotions if I were you."

It was as if cold water hit my face; I may have even choked audibly. It was ludicrously simplistic advice, but I trusted my father-in-law and did as he suggested. It was one of the best decisions of my life.

My passion for the Word of God soared, and I found that daily devotions, far from dampening the spark in my soul, further fuelled the flames of deeper personal renewal. I was no longer torn, worrying over which group would accept me, as the Spirit and the Word worked together to incline my heart towards all with equal intensity. There were hungry souls to be fed, fearful hearts to be wooed, and torrential waters of ecstatic spirituality that needed to be channelled, lest they wash away completely the bridges that God was building. Twenty-five years later, when I completed a post-graduate studies degree in seminary, I found both comfort and challenge in further blurring the "us/them" dichotomy. It was not "me," there was no "them," only "us," and it was only in that "us" that we could find *him*.

There were ebbs and flows over the years, as with any romance, but the subjective experiences of renewal continued, as did the sense of belonging, at last, to God's people. However, that sense of solidarity, as well as the charismatic gifts and manifestations, only flowed in proportion to my outward focus. I discovered that, when I sought God just for the "hit" of spiritual manifestations, my sense of his presence actually decreased, and my discernment in his gifts was shot to pieces. In that state, I did more harm than good. I worked to stay focused on serving those to whom I had been sent. I welcomed the experiential, when it occurred, heartily. But I knew that it was not meant to be just for "me," but for "us," for the whole Body. It was as if God were saying to me, "You can only come so close on your own. If you want more of me, you'll need to come with your siblings!"

There were times when I struggled with motivation, when brothers and sisters seemed more of a burden and an irritant, a hindrance to the fulfillment of my own desires. And at times I drew near to God only to have him wave me away, wanting me to finish the task at hand and come back later, when I could bring others with me.

Although the prize of intimacy with God is unquestionably worth any sacrifice, it requires choosing death to Self. Sometimes that death is dramatic and romantic. Usually, it is a drag: long, drawn out, and tedious, like trudging up and down the same mountain countless times.

CHAPTER TEN
We Are

"Slow down!" Nathan panted, tugging at his friend's sleeve. Mike shook his head, not slackening his pace.

"No way!" he shot back. "I wanna get to the top before the tourists and see the sunrise without a bunch of stupid chatter and photo ops."

"Dude. There's like a million stairs here. My calves are totally seized." Nathan winced.

"Only four thousand," Mike laughed breathlessly, continuing to leap up the stone steps. "You should have tons of energy from that breakfast you ate at the monastery. Anyway, we're almost... there!"

Stopping to stretch and catch their breath, the two friends looked around them. The sky was only now beginning to lighten as the sun rose over the Bedouin settlements in the desert below. It was a breathtaking view. Mike imagined Moses, looking out over these same plains, thousands of years before.

"So this is where the Ten Commandments were given," he murmured. "Imagine the old guy spending forty days and nights, camped up here with God."

"Yeah?" Nathan snorted. "Probably took him that long for his blisters to heal."

***

Mt. Sinai, also called Mt. Horeb, is traditionally believed to be located in the southern Sinai Peninsula. It requires approximately three hours to climb the almost 8,000-foot peak. This presumes that one is using the modern "Path of Moses," a convenient stairway of nearly four thousand steps. But those stairs would not have existed in Moses's day, and the elderly patriarch would not have had the benefit of sturdy hiking boots or Power Gel. It would have been a gruelling climb. Yet, by the thirty-fourth chapter of Exodus, it seems that Moses may have climbed Mt. Sinai as many as six times (Exodus 19–24).

He was eighty-odd years old, hardly a young man, and he must have found the climb tiring. God seems unsympathetic to any weariness Moses might have felt. In one instance, he arrived at the top only to be told by God to immediately descend, deliver some warning to the Israelites (which Moses argues, somewhat peevishly, that they are already well aware of), and then climb up again with Aaron in tow (Exodus 19:20–24). Twice, Moses camped out at the peak for forty days, while God laid groundwork for a new, divinely-designed culture over which Moses was to govern as Deliverer, Teacher, Priest, and Prophet. It is also on this peak that Moses stood in the cloud of God's holy presence, and not only survived, but interacted with God face-to-face, as a friend (Exodus 33:11). Yet friendship did not prevent God from being rather unreasonable, sending Moses back down the mountain, only to call him up again and again. Why did God put Moses through this? Why not just have him climb the peak once, get all the information he needed in a few hours, and descend before the Israelites had time to worry and resort to worshipping a golden cow?

It would seem that God was in no hurry and not overly concerned with efficiency. Just as he chose to repeat the plagues in Egypt, he chose to call Moses up the mountain several times. In Egypt, we saw, the delay of deliverance emphasized God's glory and power over Pharaoh and the Egyptian deities. It also served to whet the appetite of the Hebrew slaves, as God brought freedom just within reach, then snatched it away, and then offered it again. The lengthy process of victory gave the people a chance to buy in to the vision, strengthen their loyalty to Moses, and build the impetus of faith needed to cross the Red Sea. The prolonged, incremental deliverance acted like a kind of training ground. And now, God was taking Moses through the same process. God obviously had a purpose here, some significant growth or change that he wished to facilitate in his servant. What might that be?

All along, God affirmed Moses in his identity as one whom God is with, one whom God is sending, and one who belongs to a specific people. Is it possible that Moses had not yet fully bought in to this identity himself? Certainly, he had, until this point, done much to care *for* this people, but perhaps he hadn't yet fully identified himself *with* this people. As we have said throughout this book, our truest identity is to be found in living on mission identifying with the people to whom we have been sent. No "me," no "them," only "us." Although God had told him of his ancestral ties and his right to lead, Moses still held himself apart from the Israelites. He knew he'd been sent to them, but perhaps saw that sending as being only for the sake of completing a task. Moses had been sent so that he could become *one of them,* but was still reluctant. God brought him up and down that mountain, wearing out both shoes and patience, until a change occurred.

How do we know this? It's there, in the personal pronouns used in the text.

A CHOICE OF PRONOUNS

In the first thirty-three chapters of Exodus, not once does Moses use a personal pronoun when speaking of the Hebrews, not once does he refer to them as being "my" people. Though Moses said "let my people go" to Pharaoh, he was quoting God, not expressing himself in his own words. In every other instance, Moses calls the Israelites "this/these" people (Exodus 5:22, 23; 17:4; 32:9, 21, 31; 33:12), "the" people (Exodus 15:13; 18:15; 19:23), and "your" (God's) people (Exodus 15:16; 32:11; and twice in 33:12). What's going on?

Perhaps the constant petty rebellions, rejections, and criticisms have left Moses with war wounds that make him want to distance himself emotionally from his own people. Perhaps he has never completely gotten over the eighty years of rejection, confusion, and isolation. Whatever the reason, Moses appears to have not integrated himself into this people.

Despite everything, he doesn't see himself as one of them. In contrast, God consistently refers to the Israelites as "my" people (Exodus 3:7, 10; 5:1; 6:7; 7:4, 16; 8:20–23; 9:1, 13, 17; 10:3; 22:31). These pronouns continue for most of the book of Exodus, until the incident with the golden calf. Then the crisis of betrayal provokes a deadly conflict, and everything changes.

Near the end of Moses's first forty-day camp-out on Sinai's peak, God gives him a set of principles for this new nation to follow, astounding guidelines for the birth of a new culture meant to reflect his glory on Earth. It must have been incredible, having God cast such a vision, using the hopeless inadequacies of the mortal tongue and imagination: "*Then the Lord said to Moses, 'Write these words, for according to the tenor of these words I have made a covenant with you and with Israel'*" (Exodus 34:27, NKJV). "This is what it looks like," God seemed to be saying. "This is what holiness looks like." God describes to Moses his ways, his laws, and a system of worship that would allow for the Israelites to be his "*...treasured possession... a kingdom of priests and a holy nation*" (Exodus 19:5–6). But then, in the midst of this intensely intimate revelation of God's person and plan, comes a harsh and ugly intrusion. There's a party going on below.

The Hebrews had become convinced that Moses was dead and gone. They were agitated, and Aaron apparently panicked. They were without a figurehead, and they needed something to pull them all together. And so, they made an idol, cast from the melted gold of their jewellery, to act as a flag to which the leaderless people might rally. And rally they did, flinging aside any restraint as they indulged themselves in the kinds of self-serving pleasures that would appease the fertility gods. The people, fed up with waiting on their absentee leader, worshipped before this golden calf, committing a sin so repulsive to God that he abruptly tells Moses: "*Go down, because your people, whom you brought up out of Egypt, have become corrupt*" (Exodus 32:7).

Your people? Why has God suddenly chosen to identify his people in this way? Is he rejecting them in some way? God's choice of pronoun here seems to be intentional and, perhaps, meant to provoke a reaction in Moses. It's as if God is stepping back from his ownership of the people, washing his hands of them at last. They are no longer his people. The game has changed, the pronouns have changed, and Moses could not fail to be shocked by what comes next.

God says to Moses:

> *I have seen these people... and they are a stiff-necked people. Now leave me alone so that my anger may burn against them and that I may destroy them. Then I will make you into a great nation.*
> (Exodus 32:9–10)

Dumbfounded, Moses hears what must sound like a tempting offer. God is offering Moses the opportunity to start over, to be free of this cantankerous people, to establish the glorious culture envisioned on Sinai all by himself. He would be free to walk away from the identity confusion of his past, free to claim not just a new identity, but an outstanding destiny, just him and God. No one to criticize him, no tiresome complaints, no governmental headaches. Did his heart race at the thought? It would appear not.

Something finally seems to connect in Moses's heart. He knows that God is making no idle threat. Moses has seen God's wrath before and witnessed the ensuing slaughter at the place that memorialized the people's stubborn sinfulness. He saw the Graves of Craving. Appalled, Moses can only think, *Has it all been for nothing? Has God forgotten the promises made to Abraham? And what will the Egyptians say?* After all that Moses has gone through with this people, how could God possibly ask him to simply step aside, to walk away from them, and start over (Exodus 32:11–14)?

Pleading with God to forgive, Moses cries: "...*Turn from your fierce anger; relent and do not bring disaster on your people*" (Exodus 32:12). Moses stands up to defend the people, to protect them from God's wrath, a fire that threatens to consume them completely. But again, notice the pronoun used. They are still not "my" (Moses's) people, but "your" (God's) people. Passionate though he may be in their defence, Moses is still not one of them. Still, he cannot allow them to be destroyed. And God, heeding Moses's impassioned pleas, relents. In alarm and outrage,

Moses storms down the mountain, the two divinely-engraved tablets of the covenant law in his hands. He is met by the sound of singing:

> *Moses saw that the people were running wild and that Aaron had let them get out of control and so become a laughingstock to their enemies. So he stood at the entrance to the camp and said, "Whoever is for the Lord, come to me." And all the Levites rallied to him. Then he said to them, "This is what the Lord, the God of Israel, says: Each man strap a sword to his side. Go back and forth through the camp from one end to the other, each killing his brother and friend and neighbour." The Levites did as Moses commanded, and that day about three thousand of the people died.* (Exodus 32:25–28)

With this brutal culling of the revellers, the singing is abruptly silenced. Perhaps the people, now cowed and ashamed, hope that the deaths will atone for what they've done and appease the wrath of their God. Moses, it seems, is not convinced. The next day, perhaps fearing that a greater slaughter was yet to come, Moses climbs the mountain yet again. Once there, he pleads on their behalf. In his petitions, Moses still does not identify with the people. He again uses the second person pronoun, referring to them as "your" (God's) people. But, as he pleads, it seems that something new is happening in his heart. He's come close to seeing the people exterminated, and it has left him shaken. What if it happened again? What if God should make good on his threat? Could he bear to lose them all? Perhaps it took this crisis, coming so near to a catastrophic loss, for Moses to realize how much the people mattered to him. It is only when a thing is threatened to be taken away from us, remember, that we realize just how fervently we desire to keep it.

Moses now dares to take a bold, audacious stand before God. It's as if he crosses some line and stands in a new solidarity alongside the Israelites. He announces to God, *"But now, please forgive their sin—but if not, then blot me out of the book you have written"* (Exodus 32:32).

The moment has come. Moses is beginning to identify himself fully with this people. If God rejects them, he must reject Moses also. And if it means death, then they will die together, as one. There is no longer any "me" or "them"; Moses has become one with those to whom God has sent him. And if it means death, so be it. Though he might once have balked at sacrificing himself to deliver and lead this stiff-necked people, here Moses seems willing to embrace death on their behalf. It is a death to Self. And the result? Yet deeper intimacy with God.

UNADORNED

Moses has tasted and seen that God is good. He has heard the thunder of God's voice and glimpsed the incomprehensible beauty of God's holiness. He has stood barefoot before a burning bush, and he has lingered in friendship on a mountaintop; he knows beyond any shadow of a doubt that a relationship with God is what he wants, forever, and at any cost. Yet now he is willing to give it up. They must survive, *as a people*, or not at all. His supplication heard and heeded, Moses wins a reprieve for the Israelites, even though God strikes them with a plague to remind them of the severity of their sin and its consequences (Exodus 32:35). But in his next encounter with God, Moses is given crushing news. God agrees to spare the people, even to send an angel to guide them forward, but states that he himself will no longer personally accompany them on this journey, for they are a "stiff-necked people."

To go forward without the presence of God is unthinkable. God *must* go with them; it's incomprehensible to Moses that they might lose the tangible evidence of this relationship. The people are devastated at the prospect, and Moses is appalled. *Why spare our lives at all,* he thinks, *if we lose your presence?* The Lord is adamant. In distress, the people strip themselves of their party clothes and jewellery, and stand before their God, humbled and unadorned. Exodus 33:5 tells us that God required this of them, a tangible symbol of the kind of self-exposure and vulnerability that he desires of his people:

> *"You are a stiff-necked people. If I were to go with you even for a moment, I might destroy you. Now take off your ornaments and I will decide what to do with you." So the Israelites stripped off their ornaments at Mount Horeb.*

Yet Moses, there in the meeting tent he pitched at a safe distance outside the camp, still dares to argue with his friend. Having experienced the intimate presence of the Almighty, Moses cannot now imagine exchanging that for a God who, although sovereign and powerful, would be distant and remote. The prize would be lost.

Moses goes up into the Lord's presence and argues against this sentence, a sentence which is, for him, worse than death. There is perhaps an undertone of poignant yearning in his words: "*If you are pleased with me, teach me your ways so I may know you and continue to find favor with you. Remember that this nation is your people*" (Exodus 33:13). Moses pleads with God, reminding him of their relationship. "You say that you love me, that I am your friend," Moses is saying. "Listen to me now, for the sake of our friendship. Show me that you are loving and gracious. This is your people, you can't leave them! Do you, will you, love me that much?" Mingled with this plea for forgiveness and mercy, Moses seems to express a desire to know God more, beyond even the astounding degree of intimacy that he's already experienced.

God's response is provocative and, again, the tension is evident in the pronouns. He does not relent from his decision to withdraw from the people, but now says*: "My presence will go with you [Moses], and I will give you [Moses] rest*" (Exodus 33:14). This is astounding. God declares that he is willing to grant the intimacy of his presence to Moses alone, but he makes no such promise regarding the rest of the people. For them, it would become an "us/them" relationship with God for the rest of their lives. While God and Moses would go on walking together in companionship, sharing their hearts and thoughts with one another, the rest of the people would follow behind, bereft of any cloudy or fiery pillar. They might still fulfill their destiny as a people and reach the Promised Land. But they would not walk there *with* God, only behind him. "This is the offer," says God. "Take it or leave it."

Moses reaches a pivotal moment of decision. No deal. There can be no "me" and "them"; he and the people must be as one before God. If not, then he will not take another step, despite the longing in his heart to continue in the presence of God. It's all or nothing; all of the people, or none at all, including himself. Pay attention to the pronouns that

Moses now uses, as "me" and "them" become "us," and Moses chooses at long last to identify fully with the people that he has been leading. Moses declares, "... *If your Presence does not go with us, do not send us up from here. How will anyone know that you are pleased with me and with your people unless you go with us?...*'" (Exodus 33:15–16). Moses surrenders the last vestige of any independent identity. He will not be considered apart from the people; their fate is his fate.

And God's response is suffused with kindness: "*I will do the very thing you have asked, because I am pleased with you and I know you by name*" (Exodus 33:17). Is this what God was wanting for all along? Have the forays up and down the mountain helped to wear down the stubborn, prideful independence? Has God's ardent desire to befriend an entire community finally penetrated Moses's heart? There is a powerful affirmation in God's words, as if he were saying, "For you, Moses, for you alone I will do this thing, Yes, I care that much."

THE CLEFT OF THE ROCK
Love unspeakable, grace unfathomable. To so know, and to be so known. Dying to Self, Moses finds that he is able to come even further into God's presence, for now he is bringing the people with him. Moses plunges Self into the boundless, merciful depths of Other. He is one who belongs to God, he is one who is sent. And now, he is one who belongs to God's people. He is one for whose sake God is willing to change his mind—for him, Moses—because he has embraced the mission that moves God's heart. Overwhelmed, Moses seems to pause and take a deep breath. If God so loves him, then what are the limits? How far, how deep, can he go? Suddenly, in the face of this overwhelming disclosure of God's love, Moses bursts forth impetuously with all the longing of his soul. Longing that has, perhaps, been pent up within him since he was first set adrift, nameless and alone, in a basket of reeds on the Nile. Moses believes, receives God's favour, worships, and then dares to ask for even more: "... *Now show me your glory*" (Exodus 33:18).

Moses has surrendered Self and chosen Other. He embraces inclusion into a missional community that will, although he does not yet know it, be eternal. In doing so, he finds that it opens the way to a depth of intimacy in his relationship with God that he had never before imagined. In his moment of identity crisis, Moses chose to identify with a sinful, fretful people. He dared to pray a magnificent prayer, asking for more than any man had ever before asked, and receiving more than any man had ever before received. God replies:

> …"I will cause all my goodness to pass in front of you, and I will proclaim my name, the Lord, in your presence.… But," he said, "you cannot see my face, for no one may see me and live." Then the Lord said, "There is a place near me where you may stand on a rock. When my glory passes by, I will put you in a cleft in the rock and cover you with my hand until I have passed by. Then I will remove my hand and you will see my back; but my face must not be seen." (Exodus 33:19–23)

Moses receives a new set of blueprints for the nation of Israel, laws inscribed again in stone by God's own hand. Holiness is to be their corporate, national identity, their distinct culture. *Our* nation, thinks Moses. *Our* identity. *Our* culture. And there, on the peak of Sinai, God manifests his glory, while his friend Moses is hidden safely in a cleft in the rock. As the Lord passes by, he proclaims the identity from which all of our identities must come. He proclaims himself, he reveals himself, and he shares himself with Moses, his friend:

> …"The Lord, the Lord, the compassionate and gracious God, slow to anger, abounding in love and faithfulness, maintaining love to thousands, and forgiving wickedness, rebellion and sin. Yet he does not leave the guilty unpunished; he punishes the children and their children for the sin of the parents to the third and fourth generation." (Exodus 34:6–7)

And so Moses, having touched the prize of intimacy with God, "*bowed to the ground at once and worshiped*" (Exodus 34:8). God took Moses from nameless-ness, through rejection, into radiance. Now, as Moses comes down from being in the presence of the Lord, his face shines so brightly that the people are afraid to come near (Exodus 34:29–35). Generations to come would hold up this degree of radiance, this intimacy reflected in glory, as the highest aspiration of the human soul. Paul would write that:

And we all, who with unveiled faces contemplate the Lord's glory, are being transformed into his image with ever-increasing glory, which comes from the Lord, who is the Spirit. (2 Corinthians 3:18)

Moses's shining face foreshadows the brilliance of Jesus on the Mount of Transfiguration (Matthew 17:1–13), where the Father asserts the identity of his Son, proclaiming *"...This is my Son, whom I love. Listen to him!"* (Mark 9:7). And so, the faces of God's people are meant to shine, even in the darkest times, when death to Self seems intolerable and the prize of intimacy with God unattainable. The journey from identity crisis into missional community is the only pathway to true intimacy with God. Along the way, we learn that we can only get so close to God on our own; to come closer, we must come as a people. The way into this one-ness involves a steep and difficult climb. And the road to Sinai takes us through Gethsemane.

"AS WE ARE ONE..."

Lined up on the stage, the children seemed to draw comfort from each other and the courage to approach the microphone.

"Papa was always there for me," the eleven-year-old girl brushed back her tears. "He was the best grandfather anyone could ever have." Her brothers, sisters and cousins all nodded, equally grieved at the passing of this man who had been such a formative part of their lives.

"He left everything for us," the oldest said. "His friends, his career in Egypt, his community. He left it all to bring his children to Canada, so we could have a better, safer future."

The grandchildren went on to bear witness to the fact that this man had left an enduring legacy behind, but it was not without personal sacrifice. They recounted the story of a time when he had been offered a well-paying job, but one that would require taking frequent trips away from his family and local community in Cairo, the ones he felt he had been sent to reach. He turned it down in favour of a position that paid far less but allowed him to stay closer to family. Later, when they came to Canada he chose to see his immigration as a call to global mission, and willingly subsumed his own dreams and goals to give unflinchingly of his time and resources to those around him, and most especially to his family.

Watching the slide show, and listening to the eulogies and video clips, my mother-in-law and I overheard a young bystander whisper, "That man had no life!" This person clearly did not feel admiration for him, but pity. Mom glanced over, then turned to me.

"No life?" she whispered to me, gently amused. "He has more life than most people I know!" She waved her hand, indicating the crowded auditorium. "Just look at all the lives he is still living!"

***

Although the funeral was long and emotionally draining, it was clear that any grief expressed was eclipsed by the gratitude and love felt for the deceased. My mother-in-law was right to point out the bystander's shallowness. The man who had died had not only been one of the happiest individuals she'd ever known, but, far from losing his sense of Self, he had imparted identity to his entire extended family. They were a close-knit and loving clan who always had room at their chaotic table to adopt others into their one-ness. Reflecting ruefully on how difficult it was to assemble our own motley crew for a family meal, I quickly went from pity to envy. How many times had I sacrificed family time to pursue my own interests? How many times had I missed opportunities for one-ness because of my desire for individuation?

One-ness is at the heart of the gospel. On route to Gethsemane, Jesus knew that he was going to his death. The intimacy he had known since the beginning of time would of necessity be broken, as the Father would turn his back on the Son, condemning sin in the flesh of Jesus. Christ's identity of unending one-ness with his Father would die, along with his flesh, there on that cross. Jesus needed to die a literal death to

Self so that God could have the intimacy he desired of all humanity to himself. It was perhaps with this in mind that Jesus focused his last discourse with his friends on the theme that was most on his mind: one-ness. Like the elderly Egyptian, Jesus longed to gather his children around him and assure himself that they would be united and devoted to one another once he was gone.

In his high priestly prayer, Jesus reminds his disciples of who, and whose, they are. He reminds this band of misfits that they are to be united by their common sent-ness, their identification with the ones to whom he is sending them, and the missional nature of this new community that springs out of a new covenant.

Perhaps Jesus deliberately chooses his disciples for the very reason that they do not really fit together: tax collectors, fishermen, a zealot, a thief. They had nothing in common but Jesus, and now they are to be one: one with each other and one with those whom they hope to reach. There is no fringe, there is no inner circle. There is only a Way. It points forward, sending us outside of ourselves, wherever we are. A band of sad and sinful misfits are to become the people of God. We go into all the world, even while chafing at the awkward pauses in conversation, trusting that somehow the Message will make it through the mess. And yes, it will.

At Gethsemane, Jesus prays for us all to be one: one with God one with each other and one for the sake of the world:

As you sent me into the world, I have sent them into the world. For them I sanctify myself, that they too may be truly sanctified. My prayer is not for them alone. I pray also for those who will believe in me through their message, that all of them may be one, Father, just as you are in me and I am in you. May they also be in us so that the world may believe that you have sent me. I have given them the glory that you gave me, that they may be one as we are one—I in them and you in me—so that they may be brought to complete unity. Then the world will know that you sent me and have loved them even as you have loved me. (John 17:18–23)

Choosing a life of missional community is not without tension; unity does not assume unanimity, nor does the pursuit of one-ness mean that we will avoid all conflict. On the contrary, death to Self is painful, gritty, and real. We must keep our eyes upon the prize, at all times. What is the nature of this prize, this intimate one-ness that Jesus has with the Father? Jesus expresses it in John 16:32 by saying, "...*Yet I am not alone, for my Father is with me.*" And earlier, he asserts, "*I and the Father are one*" (John 10:30). This is not a unity that knows no conflict, for there is indeed conflict in Christ's agonized pleas in the Garden of Gethsemane. But it is a unity that values relationship above and beyond all. And conflict, far from impeding intimacy, actually demands it, for it requires that we become vulnerable.

In John 10:15, Jesus describes the nature of that relationship, saying, "*just as the Father knows me and I know the Father...*" Here is intimacy: to know and be known in the kind of vulnerable self-disclosure that begs for the cup of suffering to pass us by, knowing, deep down, that we will drink of it. Intimacy does not imply uninterrupted harmony. There may be relative harmony and peace between strangers who are indifferent to one another, but this is but a shallow unity. Moses might have enjoyed a peaceful, uneventful and blessedly short journey to Canaan had he agreed to an "us/them" relationship with the Hebrews. Instead he chose to be one of them and to die to himself for a greater prize of an intimacy with God that could be shared with all.

FATHER, GLORIFY

To journey from identity crisis into missional community is to willingly lay aside Self in favour of one-ness. This means that we must stand face-to-face and argue, as Moses did, with God on behalf of others too foolish or wilful to plead for themselves. It means to die, as Moses also did, laying down his life to lead his people as near to the Promised Land as God would permit him to go. It means to embrace mission wherever we find ourselves. It means countless painful steps up and down the mountain. It means blisters and thorns and bruised egos. It hurts. But the honest expression of our pain is a part of what draws us even closer to God and to each other. Jesus, wrestling in his spirit, asked his best friends to walk a little further with him into the Garden, so that he might draw solace from their nearness.

When Jesus said, "...*may this cup be taken from me...*" (Matthew 26:39), his request did not defy, offend, or threaten God. It was, instead, a moment of raw connection. The agony of the Father more than matched that of his Son, knowing, as they both did, what the response would be, *must* be. Jesus would drink, and he would die. It was his choice—there was always the option to walk away from the cross—for, if it were not his choice, the sacrifice would be meaningless. Yet Father and Son both knew that, in order to accomplish the purpose of salvation for humanity, the cross was the only way. Jesus endured the unbearable pain of the cross that he might bridge the unbearable pain of the void between God and humanity. Jesus confronted his destiny there in the garden—three times wrestling and groaning—while the disciples slept on in exhausted oblivion. Jesus, in anguish, entreated again and again. He did so openly, passionately, vulnerably, and sweating blood.

In the end, the cup did not pass him by, and he drank of his own free will. The conflict was real and could not be avoided. The relationship, however, survived. And the identity of Christ, deeply rooted in his identification with humanity and in his one-ness with the Father, remained complete and intact, died, and rose again.

Jesus in Gethsemane was in communion with his Heavenly Father as never before. He spent time with the twelve in the upper room, and shared bread and wine with his friends just as Moses did with the seventy elders on the mountain. There was a hushed, holy encounter in that upper room even as there must have been up on Sinai when the seventy elders realized that they had seen God, and yet had not been struck dead. (Exodus 24:1–11). Now however, one *would* die. Jesus, knowing as no man can ever know the degree to which Self must die, tells God:

...Father, the hour has come. Glorify your Son, that your Son may glorify you. For you granted him authority over all people that he might give eternal life to all those you have given him. Now this

is eternal life: that they know you, the only true God, and Jesus Christ, whom you have sent. I have brought you glory on earth by finishing the work you gave me to do. And now, Father, glorify me in your presence with the glory I had with you before the world began. (John 17:1–5)

The same glory that transformed Moses enveloped the Saviour as he walked to Golgotha. That same glory envelops each of us as we walk away from our individualism into *one-ness*. We are called to be one with those to whom we have been sent. Death to Self clothes us in glory. It is the glory of those who define success, as Abraham did, who "*[lived] by faith when they died. They did not receive the things promised; they only saw them and welcomed them from a distance, admitting that they were foreigners and strangers on earth*" (Hebrews 11:13). It is the glory of Moses, who climbed a mountain one last time to meet death mid-step, believing that it would all be worthwhile in the end. The glorious light faded from Moses's face, but not from his heart. On that mountain, he viewed the Promised Land beyond, a land that he would not enter himself, but which he already possessed. By identifying with God's people, Moses did not need to cross the Jordan in order to be one with them in taking the land beyond. He had already taken the land, with them and for them.

***

Who are we? We, the people of God, are a nation of royal, priestly, glorious misfits, called out of identity crisis into missional community. We are his Sent Ones, on mission regardless of where we are, meant to identify with his people and with those around us. Wherever we find ourselves, that is where we have been sent. And our primary identity must be that of *corporate* sent-ness, for, as individuals, we cannot truly define ourselves.

The goal of self-actualization leads to a golden calf that is deaf to our pleas and leaves us stranded in a desert of perpetual exile. Neither roles, nor relationships, nor our own ambitions can provide for us an identity strong enough to equip us to serve and lead confidently in the world. Any name we give ourselves falls far short of the name God desires to give us. Only when we relinquish the right to our individuality, and die to Self for the sake of Other, do we experience real intimacy with God and with his people. The identity that God speaks over us is that of one-ness with himself and with his Church in a single purpose and mission. It is a one-ness that must and will be challenged, again and again, until we learn to fight for it, defend it, and own it for ourselves. We may not win every battle, but we are never alone in the fight.

"I am," declares Yahweh, the unnameable one. And meeting his gaze, our hearts respond, "We are."

A PRAYER

Lord God, I confess that I have sought to find identity and fulfillment apart from you. I have pursued self-actualization and made it my idol. I have not allowed you to define me, for fear of losing my fragile sense of Self. I have not pursued intimacy with you as I might have, because the cost was too great. And for this I am truly sorry.

I confess too that I have resisted being a part of your Body here on Earth, avoided identifying with your people, and instead I have taken my identity in being either a rejected outcast, or a tragically misunderstood leader. I have comforted myself with achievement, offended you with my pride, and taken refuge in isolation. I have not sought relationship with your people as I might have, and for this I am truly sorry.

I pray that you would break these patterns of sin in my life, and that you would show me how to join with you in your mission here on earth, to be in community and to identify with those to whom you are sending me. Please heal me of the hurt and the fear of rejection by helping me find my identity as one whom you love, as one who belongs to you, as one whom you are sending, and as one of your people. Please show me who I am in your sight.

I choose to lay aside any prideful individualism and humbly ask that you show me how I can be reconciled to your people in intimate fellowship and contribute fruitfully to your Kingdom. Make us one, as you, Father, Son, and Holy Spirit, are One. May we, your people, experience your love, so that forever after our faces would shine in your presence.

Show us your glory.

Bibliography

Abada, Teresa; Hou, Feng; and Lu, Yuqian. *Choice or Necessity: Do Immigrants and Their Children Choose Self-Employment for the Same Reasons?* A Statistics Canada research paper found at: www.statcan. gc.ca/pub/11f0019m/11f0019m2012342-eng.pdf (Accessed February 2015)

Allender, Dan B. *Leading with a Limp.* Colorado Springs: Waterbrook Press; 2006.

Archer, Gleason L. *A Survey of Old Testament Introduction.* Chicago: Moody Press; 1974.

Ashby, Odfrey. *Go Out and Meet God.* Grand Rapids: Wm. B. Eerdmans Publishing Co.; 1998.

Augsburger, David W. *Pastoral Counseling Across Cultures.* Philadelphia: Westminster Press; 1986.

Berdichewsky, Bernardo. *Latin Americans Integration into Canadian Society in B.C.* Vancouver: Bernardo Berdichewsky; 2007.

Bonino, Jose Miguez, "Genesis 11:1-9, a Latin American Perspective", in *Return to Babel: Global Perspectives on the Bible.* John R. Levison and Priscilla Pope-Levison, editors. Louisville, Kentucky: Westminster John Knox Press; 1999.

Brown, C. "Hatshepsut; The King Herself." In National Geographic's feature article for April 2009. Found at: www.ngm.nationalgeographic.com/2009/04/hatshepsut/brown-text/1 (Accessed July 2015)

Crenshaw, Kimberlé. "Demarginalizing the Intersection of Race and Sex: A Black Feminist Critique of Antidiscrimination Doctrine, Feminist Theory and Antiracist Politics," University of Chicago Legal Forum: University of Chicago Law School; 1989.

Delgado, Richard and Stefancic, Jean. *Critical Race Theory: An Introduction.* New York, NY: New York University Press; 2001.

Deutsch, Amy Dolores. *Psychoeducational and Therapeutic Group Counseling for Central American Female Immigrants.* Michigan: ProQuest LCC; 2009.

Dodson, Aidan and Hilton, Dyan. *The Complete Royal Families of Ancient Egypt: A Genealogical Sourcebook of the Pharaohs.* London: Thames and Hudson; 2004.

Dueck, Abe J., Guenther, Bruce L. and Heidebrecht, Doug, editors. *Renewing Identity and Mission: Mennonite Brethren Reflections After 150 Years.* Winnipeg: Kindred Productions; 2011.

Dueck, Gil. "A Faith I Can Call my Own", in *Renewing Identity and Mission: Mennonite Brethren Reflections After 150 Years.* Dueck, Abe J., Guenther, Bruce L. and Heidebrecht, Doug, editors. Winnipeg: Kindred Productions; 2011.

Elmer, Duane *Cross-Cultural Conflict: Building Relationships for Effective Ministry.* Illinois: InterVarsity Press; 1993.

Fletcher, Joann, *Chronicle of a Pharaoh: The Intimate Life of Amenhotep III.* New York, NY: Oxford University Press; 2000.

Galbraith, John Kenneth. *American Capitalism: The Concept of Countervailing Power.* New Jersey: Transaction Publishers; 1993.

Goldingay, John. *Exodus and Leviticus for Everyone.* Louisville, Kentucky: Westminster John Knox Press; 2010.

Green, Joel B. "The Gospel of Luke", in *The New International Commentary on the New Testament.* Gordon D. Fee, editor. Grand Rapids, Michigan: William B. Eerdmans Publishing Company; 1997.

Gundry-Volf, Judith M. and Volf, Miroslav, *A Spacious Heart.* Harrisburg: Trinity Press International, 1997.

Hamilton, Victor P. *Exodus: An Exegetical Commentary.* Grand Rapids: Baker Academic, 2011.

Hauerwaus, Stanley. *Resident Aliens.* Nashville: Abingdon Press; 1989.

Heifetz, Ronald A. and Linsky, Marty. *Leadership on the Line – Staying Alive Through the Dangers of Leading.* Boston: Harvard Business School Press; 2002.

Hiebert, Paul G. and Meneses, Eloise. *Incarnational Missiology: Planting Churches in Band, Tribal, Peasant, and Urban Societies.* Grand Rapids: Baker Press; 1995.

Hopper, Tristan. "Canada: As Immigration Booms, Ethnic Enclaves Swell and Segregate", in *National Post,* February 11, 2012.

Johnstone, W. *Exodus: Old Testament Guides.* Sheffield, England: Sheffield Academic Press; 1999.

Kaminsky, J.S. "Corporate Responsibility in the Hebrew Bible", *in Journal for the Study of the Old Testament: Supplement Series 196.* Sheffield: Sheffield Academic Press; 1995.

Kirschner, David. *Adoption: Uncharted Waters: A Psychologist's Case Studies.* Woodbury, New York: Juneau Press; 2006.

Lanier, Sarah A. *Foreign to Familiar: A Guide to Understanding Hot-and Cold- Climate Cultures.* Hagerstown, MD.: McDougal Publishing; 2000.

Lartey, Emmanuel Y. *In Living Color: An Intercultural Approach to Pastoral Care and Counseling.* London: Jessica Kingsley Publishers; 2003.

Livermore, David A. *Cultural Intelligence: Improving Your CQ to Engage Our Multi-Cultural World.* Grand Rapids: Baker Academic Press, 2009.

Mancini, Will. *Church Unique: How Missional Leaders Cast Vision, Capture Culture, and Create Movement.* San Francisco: Jossey-Bass; 2008.

McConnell, Doug, Pocock, Michael, and Van Rheenen, Gailyn. *Missions: Biblical Foundations & Contemporary Strategies.* Grand Rapids: Zondervan Publishing House; 1996.

McNeal, Reggie. *A Work of Heart – Understanding How God Shapes Spiritual Leaders.* San Francisco: Jossey-Bass; 2000.

Meyers, Carol; Perdue, Leo G.; Blenkinsopp, Joseph, and Collins, John J. *Families in Ancient Israel.* Louisville, Kentucky: Westminster John Knox Press; 1997.

Milgrom, J. *JPS Torah Commentary on Numbers.* Philadelphia: Jewish Publication Society; 1990.

Neufeld, Alfred. "Recovering Apostolic and Prophetic Origins and Identity: Revisiting the Meaning of Mennonite Brethren Dissent in 1860", in *Renewing Identity and Mission: Mennonite Brethren Reflections After 150 Years.* Dueck, Abe J., Guenther, Bruce L. and Heidebrecht, Doug, editors. Winnipeg: Kindred Productions; 2011.

Nida, Eugene A. *Understanding Latin Americans: With Special Reference to Religious Values and Movements.* California: William Carey Library; 1974.

Olberg, Kalervo, "Culture Shock: Adjustments to New Cultural Environments." In *Practical Anthropology* 7:4; 1960.

Piper, John. *Do Not Be Conformed to This Word.* Sermon on Romans 12:1-2 (2004). Found at www.desiringgod.org/resource-library/sermons/do-not-be-conformed-to-this-world (Accessed Nov. 2014)

Rasche, Carl. *GloboChrist: The Great Commission Takes a Postmodern Turn.* Grand Rapids: Baker Academic Press; 2008.

Shanks, Hershel. "The Exodus and the Crossing of the Red Sea According to Hans Goedicke", *Biblical Archaeology Review* 7 (1981).

Sharone, Ofer. *Flawed System, Flawed Self.* Chicago: University of Chicago Press; 2013.

Shenk, David W. *Global Gods,* second edition. Scottsdale *Pennsylvania*: Herald Press; 1999.

Shenk, David W. and Kateregga, Badru D. *A Muslim and a Christian in Dialogue.* Scottsdale, *Pennsylvania*: Herald Press; 1997.

Steindorff, George and Seele, Keith C. *When Egypt Ruled the East.* Chicago: Illinois University of Chicago Press; 1957.

Tamez, Elsa. *Amnesty of Grace: Justification by Faith from a Latin American Perspective.* Nashville: Abingdon Press; 1993.

Taylor, Charles. *Sources of the Self: The making of the Modern Identity.* Cambridge, MA: Harvard University Press; 1989.

Taylor, Joan E. *Christians and the Holy Places: The Myth of Jewish-Christian Origins.* Oxford: Clarendon Press; 1993.

Taylor, Mark C. *Multiculturalism and Politics of Recognition.* A. Gutman, editor. Princeton: Princeton University Press; 1992.

Twenge, Jean M. *Generation Me: Why Todays' Young Americans are More Confident, Assertive, Entitled – and More Miserable than Ever Before.* New York: Free Press; 2006.

Tyldesley, Joyce A. *Hatchepsut: The Female Pharaoh.* London, EN: Penguin Books; 1998.

Van Horn, Carl (Ph.D.), Zukin, Cliff (Ph.D.) and Kopicki, Allison. "Left Behind: The Long-term Unemployed Struggle in an Improving Economy". Found at: www.heldrich.rutgers.edu/sites/default/files/products/uploads/Work_Trends_September_2014_0.pdf Accessed July 2015.

Walls, Andrew, "The Gospel as Prisoner and Liberator of Culture", in *The Missionary Movement in Christian History: Studies in the Transmission of Faith.* New York: Orbis Books; 1996.

West, Charles C. *Power, Truth and Community in Modern Culture.* Harrisburg, Pennsylvania: Trinity Press International; 1999.

Winsman, Albert L., Clifton, Donald O. and Liesveld, Curt. *Living Your Strengths.* New York: Gallup Press; 2003.

Wright, N. T. "God and Caesar, Then and Now," Festschrift for Dr Wesley Carr; 2003. Found at: www.ntwrightpage.com/2016/05/07/god-and-caesar-then-and-now/ (accessed June 2020).

Zimmerman, Jens. *Incarnational Humanism: A Philosophy of Culture for the Church in the World.* Illinois: IVP Academic; 2012.

About the Author

Nikki White writes for *MULTIPLY*, the global mission agency of the Mennonite Brethren Church. While gathering and publishing stories from all over the world, White also serves the local and global Church through teaching prayer seminars and helping in the training of short- and long-term missionaries.

The theme of identity crisis is one which White relates to on a deep, personal level. Her childhood was, like many, marred by trauma, neglect, and abuse, leaving behind emotional scars that both disfigured her and damaged others, including her own children.

Embracing an identity of sent-ness allowed God to begin weaving her brokenness into his overarching story of redemption in ways which gave profound meaning to the seemingly random chapters of her life. For White, this led her to the international mission field, to undergraduate studies in Fine Arts in Colima, Mexico, to a career in the worship arts, to graduate studies in seminary (MBBS, Trinity Western University), to a vocation in prayer counselling and life coaching, to a missionary journalism role with *MULTIPLY* and, now, to the penning and publishing of this, her first book.

White and her family attend North Langley Community Church in B.C., Canada, where she oversees curriculum development and training for prayer ministry.

Visit Nikki at www.whitestoneid.ca.